DEADBEAT MOMS (IT'S NOT JUST ABOUT MONEY)

Naomi Brunner
With Dr. Simon Casey Ph.D.

For information address
Brunner Press,
Online: Brunnerpress@aol.com

Library of Congress Cataloging-in-Publication Data
#TXu1-813-573

ISBN: 978-0-615-94614-6

Published January 2014
by Brunner Press BP

CONTENTS

§EVEN THOUGH§

Even though you slap me, push me, scratch me, I still love you.

Even though you've bit me, slammed me, yanked me, I place no one above you.

Even though you've punched me, kicked me, dragged me, I still care.

Even though I watched you hold someone else's child in your arms, I cried because I wished I was there.

Although you have admitted these things you do they're wrong, you blame the other parent, but they're long gone.

All these painful scars are bandaged slits; but your still number one on my list.

I may sound crazy for saying this, but I have forgiven you and moved on, oh but my dear my dear, you'll soon have to answer to god

A Caseworkers Perspective

Caseworkers provide great resources, but parent have to be receptive to the services. In some cases a parent may lack the knowledge of exactly what services is needed with his or her family. This is an area where it it's important that friends and professionals, such as teachers become important to a family. A recommendation of services may provide necessary care in ensuring a child survives.

The saying," It takes a village to raise a child..." really is appropriate in this line of work. As a case with limited powers it was part of my duties to ensure the safety of the children in the report before going home and getting rest. Needless to say there were countless nights spent removing children from reported dangers of neglect or abuse and placing them in foster homes or temporary shelters, where one could only hope that the abuse or neglect for these children under the age of eighteen would be able to care for themselves.

There were some success stories in many cases of foster care placements during my time at the agency, but there were also a lot of failures too. These failures had as much to do with flaws in the system as well as the friends, relatives and those close to the subject child. Friends and relatives would be enablers to the abuse or neglect by not identifying and reporting the abuse or neglect. In either case, the system breaks down whenever a child dies from being abuse or neglect by a caretaker who is ill equipped to handle the situation. Some professionals worked directly or indirectly with children and persons working in law enforcement, such as the police, and the education system, such as teachers and guidance counselors are specially trained to spot abuse and neglect of a child. But even so, a neglected or abuse child may pass by you or someone like you on a daily basis, and because the child is afraid, that child may never say anything.

In this book, Deadbeat Moms, the author, Naomi Brunner gives clear, precise guidance and lifts the veil from the cloudy area of intervention. Remember, 'children learn what they live, and live what they learn. In order to stem the abusive or neglectful behavior from being passed on to future generations then something has to be done, and there can be no better time than the present. Reading this book will give positive insight as to how to conduct interventions and getting involved with raising a child properly.

The author, who was also a product of the foster care system, offers advice on how the layman or common citizen can spot abuse or a neglected child. They are all around us. It's time for us to open our eyes and realized that our children are our future. Their wellbeing is entrusted to professionals, but everyone must play their part in ensuring their safety. Sometimes things fall through the crack and the adults around either let it happen or become immune to the activities. Always remember that your action may result in the life of a child being saved.

I'm encouraging all parents, friends of parents and everyone to read this book and keep a copy close by.

INTRODUCTION

My name is Naomi Brunner and I've been on all sides of the issues discussed in this book. I was that child, a parent…and even became involved with the so-called system. I'm not a social worker, a clinical psychologist or a researcher. I am simply someone who has experienced firsthand what it is like to grow up with a deadbeat mom-two in fact.

I grew up not wanting to follow in the footsteps of either of these women, but instead wanting to try my best to be a good mother when I had my own child. I was thrilled when she was born! I know I'm not the perfect mom, but I'm trying my best, and I've learned from my own misfortune.

It was a rough road growing up, yet somehow I managed to steer clear of the drug abuse all around me. I didn't like what it did to people. Then when I became a parent, I recognized the importance of not only caring for, but also protecting my daughter and, in several cases, the children of deadbeat moms, who needed help.

In this book, I talk about the many types of deadbeat moms, mostly from firsthand experience, learning from my years of living in urban America, New York City to be more specific. Not that anything in this book is relegated to only big cities. These stories can (and do) take place anywhere. For instance, therapist Dr. Simon Casey, who contributed to this book, provides stories from California. The problems discussed in the upcoming chapters are very real and unfortunately very widespread.

I hope that this book can be used to champion a cause, so to speak, and help stop the increase of deadbeat, neglectful and/or abusive moms. Perhaps it will get people to speak up and call Social Services more quickly if they suspect a child is being treated poorly, or even offer to help out if it is a family member of the child of someone in their life. Please pardon me if at any time I sound preachy because that is not my intent. I'm passionate about this issue. Hopefully together we can help change a system that needs to start cracking down on deadbeat moms of all kinds.

CHAPTER 1
Not Paying Their Fair Share

Financial responsibilities are usually part of the problem when it comes to the difficulties of parenting. This is common in many families in which one or two parents work long and hard to keep a roof over their children's heads and food on the table. Yet, when something goes wrong, and the money is not there for the family, it is almost always the father who gets the bad rap, while the mom rarely ever takes the blame, even if she has custody or is deemed by the courts to pay her fair share.

We're still raised to think that dads pay the bills, despite how many working moms are out there. Even being raised by a mom who could rarely ever find the money to buy anything for her children, I still didn't think it was her fault when I was very young. I guess I was, like so many young children, raised to believe our dads would take care of us.

My dad probably would have done so if my mom didn't hate him and if she allowed him to help us. In fact, when it came to the holidays my dad would try and snatch my brother and I away from her to spend time with him. Of course, she hated the fact that he would provide for us and make us happy while she was too busy spending time out on the streets doing drugs or selling them.

While many people have experienced the opposite scenario, with a mom trying to provide the family with holiday presents and a festive mood, while their dad is off somewhere, my story was all about having a deadbeat mom, actually more than one. As I grew up, I realized that if she had custody of my brother and I, then she was supposed to take some financial responsibility. She didn't. She wanted to keep us away from our father, but didn't want to provide for us. Holidays came and went and maybe she'd buy us new socks or a scarf. On birthdays, maybe I'd get a dollar or two, if I saw her on that day. My mom was often crashing at other people's houses in a drugged out state. Either that or she was running the streets, dealing or spending the night in jail. My dad, however, made a world of difference. When we were able to see him around the holidays, there were Christmas cookies. I would get new shoes or a dress while my brother would also get shoes and perhaps a new pair of pants.

One year he bought me a new coat with a muffler to put your hands in when it was cold. We'd sing Christmas Carols and on Easter he would put on a fake bunny nose and try to hop around the house and entertain us while singing Peter Cotton Tail. We would have a lot of chocolate and sometimes go to the movies.

I feel like although he didn't have much money, whatever he had, he would use to try to make us happy. Of course, there were times when he, like my mom, was also abusive, especially to my brother. But there was some sense of responsibility toward us, and even if I didn't like his curfews, when I got older and lived with him, I knew he cared so much about us.

Blame it on the Dads

I grew up in Harlem with my mom and brother, and I constantly heard the local women talking about how it was always the man's fault if life was difficult and there was no money.

Fathers had kids and then when they got bored they took off. The men were at fault for everything. It wasn't until later on that I began to understand that my mom and plenty of these other moms were deadbeats in so many ways. They were neglectful, abusive and many of them were strung out most of the time. In some cases I'm sure they were part of the reason the men left. I'm not saying it's easy to raise children as a single parent, believe me I know firsthand. BUT, I also know what it means to make an effort.

No matter how bad these women were, it was always the men who were supposed to provide for their families. Those who did not, or could not pay child support for whatever reason, were defined as deadbeat dads. Over the years I read a lot of articles about deadbeat dads and how the family courts needed to crack down on them and make them pay child support or bring them to justice. I even had to deal with my own daughter's father who fit into this category because he took off and never had enough money to send me to help raise my daughter.

Then, one day, while in the process of trying to collect money owed from my daughter's "deadbeat dad," I noticed that there were more men in court waiting to see the judge than women. In particular, I noticed one gentleman sitting with five children, whom I later found out were all his. At first I thought maybe he was there with the mother of the children and that he was watching them while she went into the courtroom. Then the court officer came out and called out Jean Smith vs. Anthony Smith. The man stood up and began walking toward the bench. As he approached the bench, he began complaining about how he was tired of getting all the children dressed and taking them out of school only to find out that their mother, once again, did not show up in court. Within minutes, he was on his way out the door with five kids following him, shaking his head and telling anyone who would listen about how difficult it was to raise five children without the $15,000 owed in back child support from their mom. His last comment before leaving the courtroom was to another man sitting quietly in the back with two children at his side. “If it was me,” he said, “I would have been arrested by now.” The other man just nodded in agreement and said, “Amen.”

A Growing Problem

I recently read about an attorney in Charlotte, North Carolina who said, “I’m seeing a lot more situations where the moms are not the ‘good guy’ anymore,” noting that moms make up 25 percent of her child custody caseload. That’s up from about 15 percent just five years ago. Unfortunately, when deadbeat moms, or deadbeat dads, don’t pay up, the state has to pick up the tab on the children, meaning that taxpayer dollars are used instead. Deadbeat moms, in the financial sense of the term, simply do not take responsibility for their children, even when ordered to do so by the state. Surprisingly, it’s not really a new phenomenon. Since moms have entered the work force there have been many who were ordered by the courts to help support their children but simply don’t do so. The number of deadbeat moms has increased over the past thirty years with the increase in women in the workforce. According to the latest U.S. Census figures, 385,000 women out of a total of 674,000, or 57 percent pay some, or all, of the money they owe for child support.

That means there are 289,000 deadbeat moms from a financial perspective. Of course this number goes largely unnoticed for several reasons. First, there are more deadbeat dads and secondly, the family courts are still quite lenient on deadbeat moms, which is one reason I am writing this book. Changes need to be made. Moms need to be held responsible. Statistics show that, as of 2010, deadbeat moms owed nearly two billion dollars in child support. The number is less than that owed by deadbeat dads, BUT it is still a hell of a lot of money.

Adding to the problem is that deadbeat moms may not have regular jobs. Some take jobs off the books so that they can claim they don't have the money to pay child support. Others move around from job to job or place to place and are hard to find. This is a problem with deadbeat dads as well. Even with the Internet and new technology, they don't always show up when searching for them. One difference, however, is that if they are found, deadbeat dads land in jail. If deadbeat moms are found, they usually claim they are not working and typically avoid jail. **A double standard, I think**.

I've also read studies that indicate that the percentage of deadbeat moms failing to pay child support to dads who have sole/primary custody is much higher than that of deadbeat dads. As of 2010, the numbers show that dads (and there are many more of them) owe 54.3 percent of the money they are supposed to pay, but deadbeat moms owe 61.5 percent.

Who Are These Deadbeat Moms?

I've met a few of these moms who fail to pay child support. Some are, like my own mom, too dependent on drugs to hold a job to support themselves, much less their children. Others are simply too enamored with themselves to recognize their own responsibility to support their children.

One private investigator says his business is up because he gets hired to track down deadbeat moms. He explains that while part of the problem is driven by a bad economy, some of it is simply that these women are focused on themselves.

"Women went back to work, earned more money, but they didn't want to pay more child support," says the investigator. He adds that many of his cases involve deadbeat moms who are starting new businesses and have actually "lost interest" in their own kids. Amazing, but true!

One category of deadbeat moms is an interesting one in that they are not completely deadbeat. In some cases they have remarried or had children in another relationship and are sharing the financial responsibilities with their new partner. While this does not mean they can forget about their other children, they do. While my own mother was never ordered by the courts to pay child support since we were "living" with her (when she was home and when we were not dumped at the home of one of her friends, or drug dealer buddies), she did not want to spend any money on her own children.

After being sent to foster care and also living with our father, my brother and I returned to her to find that she was supporting another family. It was not her family, but the family of a friend she had met while in jail.

It was weird when my brother and I returned to her around Christmas when I was about fifteen. She bought presents for the other family but had almost nothing for us. Not only did my mom fail to provide for us while doing everything for her new family, but also when things started disappearing from our home, such as toys, clothes and money, she blamed my brother. She accused him of stealing and refused to take his word of innocence over that of her newly founded family. He was about twelve years old at the time and she hit him several times with her belt, slapped him and made him climb down the fire escape to leave the apartment.

Months later, her friend, the mother of the other children in this "new family" told my mom that her daughter and her daughter's boyfriend, both of whom were drug addicts, were the ones stealing the stuff to sell it on the street. She never even apologized to my brother, which would have cost her nothing

I'll talk more about this story of a new replacement family later in the book, but it is not uncommon for a deadbeat mom to move on and start fresh with a new family, leaving her first children in the dust. While I do understand that people separate, get divorced and start a new life, and even have a new family, it does not give that person (mom or dad) the right to completely shirk all of their responsibilities to their previous family. Nevertheless, that is what many deadbeat moms do.

One story I heard came from a couple who raised their grandchildren for nearly a decade because the mom had started another family with whom she was living the "good life."

While occasionally seeing her children, she provided no child support. As someone named Chuck wrote to me on my website, "You just can't walk in and out of your kid's life and think that that's right 'cause you feel like today you want to be a parent. It's an everyday thing just like breathing, something you have to do all the time." Chuck is so right. Yet deadbeat moms seem to get away with doing just that, making an occasional appearance in the lives of their children while not taking any responsibility.

It's also interesting that many deadbeat moms just assume that if the dad, the grandparents or another relative is now taking care of the children that they no longer need any help. This couldn't be farther from the truth. Leaving kids with relatives or grandparents doesn't mean that they have the extra money to take care of the children.

Many dads, mine was one of them, struggle to get by. In today's tough economic times money is tight and there are plenty of two income families. Raising kids is expensive, so if a parent is a deadbeat, the other parent or relatives are stuck with a great financial burden.

Going After Them

Sadly, there are too many situations in which moms manage to get a free pass in the family welfare system because they are, after all, “moms” and are supposed to be caregivers (even if they aren’t).

Cases of neglect, abandonment and abuse slip through the cracks on a regular basis. But, in the cases where the courts have ordered deadbeat moms to pay up, the law enforcement officials explain that they are making it their job to do something about it.

An attorney in Charlotte stated in a magazine article, “Moms and Dads are on equal footing when it comes to custody cases in North Carolina. Women receive no legal preference.” I have no idea whether that statement is true for other states, but stories do indicate that there are law enforcement officials trying to track deadbeat moms down.

I read one story about a deadbeat mom who ran into the closet when she saw the authorities coming to her house. She then climbed through a trapdoor under a filthy carpet and made her way through an air vent out of the house and into the backyard. The police were not fooled. They were in the backyard waiting and then arrested her. Did the courts make her pay what she owed?

Did they put her in jail? Did they let her off with nothing but a warning? The story did not say.

Another story is about a lawyer from California who was denied a passport because she was $30,000 behind in child-support. Instead of spending money on visiting her family in Mexico or on business, the appeals court ruled that the money should go to her kids. Meanwhile, warrant officers in southwest Florida, in effort to list the area's top deadbeat moms who owed up to $19,000 in child support, dubbed their initiative "Operation Father's Day" as they went out looking for these moms. Included on the list were several deadbeat moms who owed $16,000 to $19,000. The authorities asked people in several counties if they had seen them.

Even when deadbeat moms are apprehended, there is the reality that some of them simply don't have much, if any, money as they often earn less than deadbeat dads. These moms simply can't afford to pay child support. Geraldine Jensen, president of the Association for Children for Enforcement of Support, points to the studies which show that the average income for non-custodial moms is only $15,000 a year, whereas non-custodial dads average about $40,000 a year. But Ms. Jensen still says that's no excuse, and adds that they should still have to pay whatever they can. This is true since deadbeat dads who have lost their jobs and have no income are still arrested for non-payment.

While the authorities continue to track them down, it is still hard to find and bring deadbeat moms to justice. I've heard far more stories of dragging the dads into court, taking money out of their paychecks or even sending them to jail. The courts still find it easy to assume that the dad does not want to take care of his kids even if he has the best of intentions. Some dads point to the idea of being innocent until proven guilty and point out that if you are a dad without money you are immediately considered guilty of shirking your financial responsibility, which may not at all be your intention. This certainly is not the case with deadbeat moms. I have not heard of many stories where a deadbeat mom is fined or thrown in jail for the same offense. I believe in equality, that men and women should receive equal pay for the same job and have the same rights and opportunities. BUT, I also believe that they should receive the same punishments for not carrying out their responsibilities and if that means paying their fair share for the sake of their families, than that is what they should be obligated to do. It still appears, in many cases, that the same old bias remains…dads are deadbeats while moms are simply doing their best to care for their families. This is not necessarily the case.

Tip of the Iceberg

Not spending money on the welfare of your own children is only the tip of the iceberg. There are several problems underneath the surface. As noted earlier, these are the problems we talk about throughout the remainder of this book including abuse, neglect and exploitation.

Money is almost always part of a larger problem. Many of these moms are unable to share love, warmth, or anything else with their children. Some believe that they were deprived in their own childhood, or as adults, and cannot bring themselves to do better for their children.

"Why should my children have things that I did not have?" That's a characteristic thought of the deadbeat mom. They are also typically resentful of the men with whom they have children and when it comes to money, they still have the idea that the men caused all of the problems, and since they are at fault they should pay all of the money. As I mentioned earlier, I heard this time and time again from women in the neighborhoods in which I grew up who had children to raise and hated the "good for nothing" fathers. I've had my own battles with my daughter's father and while I do not blame him for everything, I want him to pay his fair share.

BUT, I also take responsibility and have worked hard to give my daughter the best life I could give her. I know that if I were in a situation in which I did not have custody of her I would still do whatever I could do for her. I knew from neglect and abuse but unlike some moms who pass that along to their children, I never wanted my daughter to grow up like that. As a single mom, I am responsible for her and that is how millions of single parents feel. If only we could instill that in the others.

It's actually all pretty simple. If you truly love and care about your children you will do whatever you can for them, whether they are living with you or not. I'd personally feel badly about myself if I did not do my best for my daughter, and that includes spending money when I can to buy her what she needs. Deadbeat moms need to be responsible and if they don't understand that on their own, then the authorities must make it clear.

CHAPTER 2

More Neglect: Something's Never Change

I recall sitting at home as a young girl, watching Casper the Friendly Ghost on our old black and white television. It was the early '70s, and I shared a bedroom in our small Harlem apartment with my older brother, Kenny. I was about three at the time and he was seven. On this particular night I smelled smoke and turned to look for my brother only to find that the fire was coming from the bed I was sitting on and Kenny was still standing there holding the match. I jumped up and ran into the hallway yelling "Fire!"

One of our neighbors, Katrina, also smelled the smoke and came out into the hall. She called the fire department and I watched as half a dozen firefighters poured into our tiny apartment and put out the fire. I clung to my doll as I stood in the hall with my brother and our neighbor.

Kenny had lit the mattress on fire on purpose. At the time I'm not sure I understood why, but as we grew up, I realized that it was because he knew she was coming home, and he wanted her attention. As it was, our mom was hardly ever home. Kenny explained to me that she was out on the streets selling drugs or in and out of police holding cells, or jail. I didn't understand too much of it, but I knew what jail was from television.

It was Katrina who gave us snacks whenever she could, knowing we were hungry, going without food for long stretches at a time. My mom hardly ever fed us, never washed our clothes and spent most of her time sleeping when she was home. Kenny, bolder than I was, would wake her up and ask her for food. She would usually ignore him and if he persisted, she'd just smack him. I would grab bread if we had it and eat it with mayonnaise.

The fire did get my mother's attention but only long enough for her to beat my brother, which was not unusual. However, things would soon be different. For a few days after the fire we stayed with Katrina, which wasn't bad because we were actually fed on a regular basis. I'm not sure if her sandwiches were really all that good or if I was just so hungry that they tasted great to me. Then, a few days later, life would change for Kenny, and for me.

The holding cells where our mom would end up after being picked up for selling drugs, was either downtown Brooklyn or downtown Manhattan, She was in and out of jail constantly.

Apparently this time, however, our mom was being sent away to jail for a longer time than usual. She had obviously topped her usual minor offenses and was sentenced to two and a half years in prison. She told the courts that she had two young children living with her neighbor; perhaps hoping the courts would be more lenient. Fortunately for us, they were not.

She was sentenced to serve her time at the Bedford's Correctional Facility for Women in Westchester County. Years later, Jean Harris (a.k.a. the Scarsdale Diet Doctor killer) and Amy Fisher, the teenager who shot her married boyfriend's wife, would also be sent to the same facility.

My brother and I were brought to a nunnery, which wasn't far from our home in upper Manhattan. We had passed this large brick building before, but I never knew what was inside. I remember a police officer coming to take us from our neighbor's apartment to the nunnery. At first I thought maybe he was taking us to jail, but I was relieved when we got to the building and saw a nun waiting for us. She introduced herself as Sister Elizabeth. She took us in, gave us food and showed us where we would be staying. She was soft-spoken and very gentle in her manner. I liked her, but Kenny did not. He simply did not want to be there. Even at seven years of age he was already getting used to being out on the streets and wanted to be on his own. Not me, I just wanted to explore our new home.

Staying at the nunnery was wonderful. It wasn't very long before I started wishing Sister Elizabeth were my mother. She was kind and never yelled or threatened to hit us. There were a few other kids, around our age and we all seemed to get along. No one fought, no one was angry. They all seemed to be happy living there. We prayed in the mornings, went to school with the sisters, had lunch with Sister Elizabeth and sat around her in a big circle talking about our families and how much we missed them, even if it wasn't entirely true. We would read the bible, play, eat dinner and go to sleep in our own beds.

Sometimes we would go to the park, on picnics or to the schoolyard to play. All of this was new to me. I remember that she gave us clothes to wear, nothing very new or fancy, but always clean and fresh. This was also new to me. I was used to wearing old clothes that got dirty and were rarely ever washed.

Once a week we would drive with Sister Elizabeth up to the Bedford facility to visit our mom in jail. We would sit with her for a little while and talk. I can't lie; there were times when we visited my mother that I couldn't wait to leave. But there were also times I would drop down to my knees begging to stay a little longer just to be closer to her. When the visits were over, Sister Elizabeth would be in her car waiting for us to come out of the prison, and it seemed that every time I got in the car the same song would come on the radio.

"I want to hold you till I die, till we both break down and cry, I want to hold you, till the fear in me subsides" (Sometimes When we Touch – Dan Hill ©1976)

I always thought that song was meant for my mother and I. Later, I would cry myself to sleep.

My mother was released from prison on good behavior after serving only two years of her sentence. The years had passed by very quickly and when it was time for her to come for us and for us to leave Sister Elizabeth, I didn't want to go. Sure I wanted to be with my mother, but the life I had come to know in the nunnery, and the way Sister Elizabeth had treated us, was so much better than my life at home with my mom. Sister Elizabeth was a stranger who took care of me in a way that I'd never been cared for before.

I was six and I just wanted the same life I had enjoyed for the past two years, playing in the park, sleeping in a comfortable bed, wearing clean clothes and eating regular meals. When I left the nunnery, I knew I would never forget Sister Elizabeth and to this day she holds a special place in my heart.

"I'm sorry. I will never put you through this again."

Those were the same words my mom stated over and over again while she continued to do the same things she was doing before she went to jail, selling drugs and hustling whatever she could get her hands on. The only thing that changed was that rather than using the drugs up her nose, she began to use them in her arms.

She would constantly try to hide her arms so that we couldn't see the needle marks, but we could see them anyway. While she was preoccupied with self- destruction, we were being taken care of by someone named Lynn, whom my mom had met while in jail.

Lynn was a mom with two boys, one named Big E and the other called Chip. We never knew what their real names were. Lynn had an apartment in Brooklyn and this is where the state agreed that my mom, my brother and I could stay since we had lost our previous apartment. Lynn was a very good mom, trying her best to take care of her boys while making sure they were fed and had clothes to wear. But she had her own drug problems and together with my mom, their costly addiction was a recipe for disaster.

There were constant smoked filled nights with the smell of drugs, and plenty of strangers coming in and out of the small apartment. The kitchen table was filled with 50-cent beer cans, and a bunch of men would always be hanging out drinking beer while waiting for their hits.

When someone couldn't get a hit, a fight would always break out. There were plenty of fights, plenty of drugs, and plenty of neglect for us kids. As bad off as Lynn was with her own problems, my mother was always worse. At least Lynn still tried to look out for her boys. My mother on the other hand looked out for herself. The drug use in the apartment got so bad that Lynn asked my mother to leave. So, with nowhere else to go, we were out on the streets, hungry, not in school, looking for someone to take us in. Actually, we did have somewhere to go, but unfortunately we never went. My dad was living at his mom's house, which was not far away in the Bedford Stuyvesant section of Brooklyn. But my mom didn't trust him and did not want us to be with him. He was a big man, about 6'4" and according to my mom, "very dangerous". I never knew exactly what he did for a living, but he was menacing and he always carried a gun. My mom told us that being with him wasn't safe. Of course being out on the streets with no food and no place to go wasn't exactly safe either. Nonetheless, she would not let him take us to his mom's home.

When it came to Kenny and me, we were always in the middle of an ongoing tug of war between them. I'm not sure why my mom wanted to hang on to us since we were clearly a burden to her, constantly having to find places to drop us off or leave us. She was completely neglectful but out of stubborn pride did not want our dad, or our grandmother, to take care of us. The few times I got to see my dad, he would ask us where she had been taking us and if we were safe. I didn't really have to answer since the neighborhoods were very close and other people would fill him in on what was going on with my mom and how she was always out somewhere without us.

We ended up staying with another one of my mom's friends who was also living in a nearby section of Brooklyn. Her name was Nana and she had four kids of her own, but she never had a problem trying to help my mother out. She would share her kids' dinner with us, give us old clothes and even enrolled us in school. Again, Kenny and I hardly ever saw our mom while we stayed at Nana's house. We went to school but didn't make many friends since nobody really knew us. I kept quiet most of the time and just did the best I could.

Living at Nana's was okay for a couple of months until her boyfriend started hanging around. On a couple of occasions, while Nana was busy around the house, her boyfriend started touching me in an inappropriate manner. I told Nana about it but she didn't believe me and told my mother that she had to find another place and take us out of her house. I think deep down inside she knew I was telling the truth about what had taken place. This time my mom went to social services and asked if they could help us find a room or an apartment. They made it clear that it would take some time. She knew that my father's family was only two blocks away from Nana's house and she also knew that if she didn't find a place soon, people would tell him that they had seen us in the area and he would be coming to take us from her.

Waiting for Public Assistance

While waiting for help from public assistance, we had to sleep in an abandoned building with other drug addicts. The place was something out of a horror movie with creaking floors, busted up walls, and wide-opened ceilings. It was the worst place for my mother to take us. Remember, I was only about six years old at the time and my brother was only nine. She trusted a homeless woman that she'd never met before to watch us while she ran the streets for money for food and drugs.

One night, after a few days of living in this shell of a building, I was awakened by the sound of my mother and some man yelling at each other. He was upset about the drugs she had sold him. She was yelling for him to get out of her way. My brother ran to help her but by the time he got to her she had already been hit in the face and was crying and praying to God for help.

The following night I heard another man yelling. This time, however, he was calling my name and my brother's name. It was our father. Friends in the neighborhood had informed him that they had seen my mother running the streets and that my brother and I were living in the abandoned building. They told him that he'd better get us out of there, so he came looking for us. My brother told me to be quiet. He was scared of our father, but I wasn't. Nothing could be worse than our mom leaving us in this hellhole. So, I yelled for my father and told him that we were in the building. He was my Superman, there to rescue us. But as we tried to leave the building, our mother was coming up the block. She saw us and starting running up the block, screaming, "No, you cannot take my kids!" She tried to grab us away from him but he was strong and yanked us away from her. I was ready to go with him regardless. He told her that if she wanted to live on the streets she could do so, but without us. Once again my mom told him that he could not take us, but he would not listen. She blocked our path and when he turned to take us in another direction, she moved in front of us again.

Finally, as she reached once again to pull us away from him, my father told her in a firm but quiet manner to kindly move out of the way or he would shoot her. She didn't move away, in fact she went to grab us again. At this point he pulled out the longest gun I had ever seen in my life, and shot her. She fell to the ground then he grabbed our arms and pulled us away. All I could remember was my mom lying on the ground.

My father found out from friends that my mother was rushed to the hospital with wounds that were not very serious. I remember my father crying. I'm not sure if it was because he shot my mother or because he knew his days of freedom were now numbered and it would be a long time before he would see us again. I remember him hugging us and telling us how we looked like him. He would tell me how I had his nose, and how my brother had his eyes and that everything would be fine.

Looking Back

It was never fine. Years later my brother and I would once again be living with her. But things didn't change. In between, my father took us to stay with friends of his in Tennessee. He was later arrested for kidnapping and attempted murder. We ended up in foster care for a while.

My mom was truly a deadbeat mom, completely neglectful when it came to raising her children. Hers was a life that had no room for children. It was a life of drugs and hustling, which she could never seem to escape. In fact, she's still hustling today.

I always wished we could just have been a happy family.

I met many kids who enjoyed a good family dynamic even if they were struggling to get by. It was all about priorities and my mom never had her priorities straight. The drugs and sheer anger had taken control of her life. My dad might have been dangerous to the rest of the world, but I think he really wanted to protect us. He couldn't stand how our mom took care of us, or actually didn't take care of us. She knew she couldn't make us happy but she was obsessed with not letting him be the person to raise us.

Mom was scared that he would do a better job and that he might actually make us happy. If only she had taken the energy she spent keeping us away from him and used it to take care of us, she might have done okay. We weren't really asking for much.

When my dad died, she didn't even let me know. I was living on my own by then, but she didn't tell me, I found out from people in the neighborhood. I never got to say goodbye to him at his funeral, and I hated her for that. And I think she hated me for loving my dad.

Deadbeat Dependent Addictive Moms

Dr. Simon Casey, who has practiced psychology in California for more than two decades, and has vast experience working with neglectful and abusive parents, points out that while genes may play a small role in why some deadbeat moms turn out to be such abusive parents, it is environment (or nurture in the "nature vs. nurture" debate) that is the primary cause of such human suffering.

He seemed awfully familiar with my story and adds that; "The story of Naomi's mom is a more common occurrence than what most people think. Although there are many deadbeat moms, deadbeat dads have always been in the spotlight."

After many years of dealing with addictive, self-destructive personalities, it became very evident to Dr. Casey that there are two types of deadbeat moms with very specific characteristics: The Sociopath mom and the dependent/ addictive moms, whom he writes about below:

Addictive women suffer overwhelming pain and abandonment issues. Unlike sociopath mothers, they are able to feel but refuse, or are unable to act on their feelings appropriately. They become addicted to chemical substances precisely because of their need to numb their feelings. Most dependent mothers initially bond with their children based upon their concept of bonding unless the child is a mistake and truly unwanted. Their best intentions to provide some nurturing and love are often compromised by their drug use, and where they are in their addictive cycle. Dependent moms tend to be self-destructive by nature and their concept of love is built around the belief of distance, distrust, guilt, shame, abuse and emotional numbness. They perceive this dysfunctional way of bonding with their children as "normal".

The other key factor with the addictive mothers is that their drug of choice is their primary and most important relationship and often there is no room for anyone else. As the addiction progresses, addictive moms lose their ability to emotionally connect. Addicted deadbeat moms do not feel much remorse or guilt about neglecting or abusing their children since they become completely consumed by their drug of choice and the most important element in their world; “the next high”. What most people don’t understand is that the addiction inhibits the natural process of emotions and their ability to bond. This explains why most addicts tend to be immature and unable to grow. In some cases it is clearly evident to see that a child is raising a child.

Neglect may not always be the result of drug addiction, but it is always damaging to the children who have to go without nurture, protection and love from their mother. From my time spent in the nunnery, I learned that life could be better. So, it was hard to understand how my own mother could not make an effort, even as her friend Lynn was doing, to take care of her own children. Even after being in prison and later having my brother and I placed in foster care, she still never changed.

I’m hoping that someday children’s services and the authorities will mandate that deadbeat mothers either take responsibility for their children or relinquish custody and even bypass foster care, letting children be adopted into families that actually want to raise them. Sadly the current process takes a long time and mothers, no matter how bad they are, get second, third and fourth chances. Many continue to screw up again and again.

During this time, it is the children who suffer since they don't stop growing up while the judges and the courts take months to make decisions. Social service agencies need support in the form of volunteers, money and favorable laws to help them move children out of seriously neglectful and potentially dangerous situations with deadbeat moms. The sooner they can make decisions and find good homes for these children the fewer kids will grow up with stories like mine.

Another Story of Neglect

Deadbeat moms often follow a similar life pattern. Dr. Simon Casey provides us with one more story of neglect from a woman that he's counseled named Annette. Hers is a story about a neglectful deadbeat mom named Nicole.

As a teenager, Nicole struggled with abandonment issues and even suicidal issues brought upon primarily because of the deaths of her parents when she was young. Both were drug addicts and died of overdoses. She had no closure from the deaths of her parents and the only parental influence in her life came from her grandmother. She also suffered from manic depression.

Her lack of a father figure led her to look for someone to fill the void. Starting at about thirteen she would get into relationships with boys and become very dependent on them. She continued to have bad relationships and when things were not going the way she had hoped, she'd become unfaithful, always hoping the right guy would come along to take care of her. Apparently he never did, so she went from boyfriend to boyfriend never being satisfied. Within a few years she became pregnant and moved in with her latest boyfriend. She immediately showed a lack of concern about the baby by smoking and drinking through the full term of the pregnancy. The baby later showed signs of heart and nerve problems that may have been from the smoking and drinking.

Only a few months after the baby was born, the couple got into a major fight and she yelled to the father that the baby was not even his. At first he thought she was just saying this out of anger but when she could not look him in the eye and tell him it wasn't true, he went to get a DNA test done. When the results came back it turned out that she was right, the baby was not his. She had cheated on him as she had done with all of her boyfriends. That was the end of the relationship. Living on welfare with custody of her baby boy, Nicole began showing signs of abuse and neglect. The baby was never bathed on a normal schedule. She was still a heavy smoker justifying her smoking by saying, “oh the windows are open, the fan is on and that the smoke is not going to affect the baby”. When the baby was nearly four months old, she got pregnant once again with another guy. She continued her bad habits through this pregnancy as well. This time she had a baby girl.

Meanwhile the baby boy was past the age of one and just starting to walk. He was, like most children, curious, yet she rarely ever gave him anything to play with, since she did not want to clean up after him. She was still going out with different men and would even have sex in front of the two babies.

When she thought her little boy, of about eighteen months was “disobeying her” she would hit him on the back of the head. She would call him expletive names that no mother should ever say to their child. To make matters worse, she would never wash the kid’s clothes. If she didn’t want to hear the child crying she would cover the little boy’s mouth with her hand and tell him to shut the f--k up. The little boy was starting to have issues. He had a hard time falling asleep and did not want to be close to his mother. When he did sleep he would wake up in the middle of the night screaming.

She had a way of putting her children to sleep by putting her hand on their heads and restraining them from moving or getting up. She would force the child to keep a pacifier in their mouth by keeping her hand on the pacifier, and applying pressure for it to stay. She may have even used a drop of Benadryl to put the child to sleep. Both children were always in wet diapers to the point that they were getting wounds on their private areas. Neither child was on time with their immunization shots.

Nicole neglected her children for men, her cell phone, cigarettes and drinking. She drank alcohol when she was able to afford it and smoked marijuana once in a while. Her children were never given any ounce of unconditional love from the woman. It's as if they were only there for the welfare money and her image of keeping the title "mother". She was unable to maintain a steady lifestyle, so she would ask Annette if she could stay with her son until she had a stable home to bring him back to. He began to stay with Annette more often. One day, they went and got a contract signed and notarized stating that Annette would have temporary custody for six months until Nicole had a stable environment for the child. At the time Annette was living in Seattle, Washington and Nicole was living with her daughter in different hotels in California.

Now she was exhibiting the same pattern with the baby girl that she did with the boy, who Annette was trying to teach to talk and was holding at night until he felt safe. When Annette saw the little girl she was always in a playpen where Nicole left her most of the time. If she cried too much the mother would throw pillows or blankets on her to keep her quiet. Thank goodness she didn't smother her.

Annette finally fully adopted the baby boy, but when she saw Nicole with the little girl, who was about two at the time, she was taken back by how Nicole was treating her. She would pull the girl by her arm and nearly drag her down the street as she walked. The pain on the little girl's face clearly showed that she was a very unhappy child. She never took a photo where she was smiling. She had no verbal skills either. Fortunately, the little girl's father had stayed in touch with Nicole and at one point he took her back to California to be with him rather than such a neglectful mom. .

Annette knew so much about Nicole's story because, as much as it pained her to admit it, she is Nicole's older sister.

"She never paid any child support for any of her children nor does she have any type of communication with them," says Annette, adding that, "as far as I am concerned my sister has no business having children. She still struggles with depression and suicidal issues and is unfit to be a parent. She now wants to move back to California and stay with the father of her little girl. It is very clear to me that the cycle of abuse and neglect we were raised in was passed along to the next generation. I already see the strange and out of control behaviors her kids are exhibiting. Yet, I did not pick up on the same tendencies that she did.

We are sisters, but I overcame the hardships of our youth. Despite my own problems and troubles I still find that a child needs love and care. It was if ingrained in me because I wanted to provide that. I tried to pass along some advice, some suggestions and the phone numbers of people I thought could help her, but my sister never saw anything wrong with her lifestyle, which was, and still is, as a deadbeat mom.

“Being deadbeat feels natural,” says Annette of her younger sister Nicole. "I wish I could change her but I can't. If I could figure out how to afford it, I'd love to adopt her other two children. If nothing else, maybe I can find someone else to adopt the children, and talk her into it. That won’t be easy, but as I mentioned earlier, I don’t think she should be allowed tor raise any children.”

CHAPTER 3

My Deadbeat Foster Mom

Abuse & Unacceptable Silence

In 1994, I worked in the child welfare system in New York City. My job was as a computer consultant, teaching classes of social workers how to enter and retrieve cases on their computers. While I was not, and am not, a social worker, I respected the work that they did and the burden they had to deal with, being understaffed and underfunded. At that time, each of roughly 200 caseworkers in that location had about thirty or forty cases to visit in an eight-hour shift. It was practically impossible for them to get to every one of those assigned cases. And what made it worse was that the next day there would be another stack of cases on their desk. If they didn't have to make an emergency removal they would then have to make comments on all of the children they checked on, and their supervisors had to read through and sign off on their reports.

There were plenty of "debates" between supervisors and caseworkers about whether or not all of the children were checked on. From my own experiences, I was pretty sure they were not getting to all of the kids they were supposed to see. When supervisors found this out they would terminate the social workers. Others would quit because the caseload was overwhelming.

This only exasperated the problem further as there were more cases, less social workers and fewer children being checked upon to see how they were doing in a foster home or in their home with their mother, or parents.

I remember one day when I noticed my niece and her mom entering the social service building. My niece had bruises all over her face but the workers allowed her to go home with her mother because their load of cases was already more than they could handle and they could not find time to help them. It was a bad system then, and the caseload and underfunding hasn't gotten any better since.

What is Foster Care Supposed to Be?

The foster care system is designed to provide temporary homes for children who are being abused and/or neglected at home or do not have someone (as in a relative) who can provide proper supervision. Often drug or alcohol abuse or financial hardship or illness (mental or physical) on the part of the biological parent(s) necessitates the need for a child to be placed in foster care either voluntarily by the parent(s) or by order of the court.

As for the foster parents, they are supposed to take responsibility for the care of the child for as long as is decided by the court and in agreement with the biological parents. Basically, they are temporary caretakers who are supposed to provide a safe environment for the children. Most foster parents, from what I have heard and read, do a decent job. They take responsibility while not becoming overly attached since this is usually a temporary situation. The children are often moved from home to home. In some cases if the courts free the child for adoption, the child will have a more suitable and permanent situation.

Foster parents take classes and are trained before being able to have a child placed in their home. Some are diligent about their training and others go through the motions. Below are a few of the responsibilities for foster parents in New York State. They are supposed to:

- Provide temporary care for children, giving them a safe, stable, nurturing environment.
- Cooperate with the caseworker and the child's parents in carrying out a permanency plan.
- Understand the need for, and goals of, family visits and help out with those visits.
- Help the child cope with the separation from his or her home.

- Provide guidance, discipline and as many positive experiences as possible.
- Set a positive example.

The problem is that all of the above items are hard to monitor in a society that with too many unscrupulous individuals who do not follow the rules. We've heard about rouge cops who shoot unarmed people or beat them up, like they did with Rodney King in the 1990s. We've read about teachers, priests and other trusted individuals who are sexually abusing young boys or girls. Fortunately, these are the exceptions to the rule, but they are out there and if left unmonitored, they can do more harm than good. The same holds true for the foster parents.

My Road to Foster Care

As I mentioned earlier, my childhood was spent mostly with my brother and my mom, when she bothered to come home. She was busy taking drugs or selling them most of the time. I actually became skilled at counting and adding numbers from her throwing rolls of money at me and asking me to count them for her. It was drug money, but at the time I didn't know that or simply didn't care.

My parents were always battling over who should be taking care of us. My mom had custody but my dad hated the way she treated us. She, on the other hand, didn't want him to have us, mostly out of spite.

At one point in their usual chess game, my dad decided to take us away from her. He knew she was leaving us with so-called friends on the streets while she went off to sell drugs. So he took us. Even though he was technically kidnapping us, he thought he was doing the best thing for his children by getting us away from her. Unfortunately, as it would turn out, he was so very wrong.

He took us all the way to Nashville to the home of some friends of his, or so he thought. He had been spending time with the Muslims whom he felt were his "brothers", at Temple # 9 in New York City. This had begun in the early 1970s with the Honorable Elijah Muhammad. We had gone with him to a couple of meetings or services when we were young and I even remember once meeting Muhammad Ali. My father was swaying back and forth, deciding whether or not to become a Muslim, which was becoming very popular at the time. I know his intentions were good. He had positive experiences with the Muslims over several years, so he believed that the couple we would be staying with were good people.

When we met them, they appeared to be very nice. They were a couple in their late thirties, or they could've been in their early forties. We were told to call him Cousin Jamal and to call her Sister Lyn. They wore some of the traditional Muslim clothing and headwear that we had seen others wearing in New York. At first I thought living with them would be a nice change from the city, out in the more beautiful country, but it didn't take long for things to become very ugly.

Cousin Jamal began beating my brother and I. His wife clearly knew what was going on but was too scared to help us. After a while I got tired of his abuse so I tried to fight back.

They had a spiral staircase and I remember trying to fight him but he grabbed a large paddle from the old days that was used for spanking. I ran up the stairs and kept falling, scraping my legs.

He yelled at both of us, "You guys want to fight me?" I remember him hitting me across my back. I guess my brother was trying to help me, so he hit him and threw him on the floor. I got up and tried to lunge toward him but he hit me so hard in the face and on top of my head that it left a big gash. I remember the blood running down my face but nobody ever took me to the hospital.

I'm not sure if he raped my brother, but I know I was, and I was nine at the time. We both wanted to run away, but we were somewhere in the middle of Tennessee and had no idea where to go. If we had been in New York we could have found our way around the neighborhood or gotten on a subway. Here, we would have needed a vehicle or something else to run away in. We had no idea if there was even a train in the area. I just kept hoping and praying the abuse and rapes would stop. We were very scared and intimidated. My dad would call to check up on us, but Jamal would always tell him we were fine and busy playing or something so that we wouldn't get on the phone. Even if we did speak to him, with Jamal there, we were too scared to say anything, knowing that he would beat us, or worse.

My mom must have reported that we were missing because eventually the FBI came looking for us. The first time they came to the door we heard them asking for us but Jamal told us to stay quiet or he'd kill us. The second time the FBI came into the house, there were no more questions, and they found us.

Cousin Jamal and Sister Lyn were arrested, but I don't know if he was ever charged for all of his crimes. My father was arrested too for kidnapping us. When we finally returned to New York we ended up back with our mother. She took us to see our father in jail mostly to show that she had custody of us again. The chess match continued.

She was not particularly upset about what had happened to us, just happy to see that he ended up in jail. But when my dad asked us if it was better with her then it was down there, we told him what had happened. It was the most devastating day of his life.

He wanted to protect us from our mother and the danger she put us in here in New York so he tried to take us to a safer place. He trusted his Muslim friends and he wished he hadn't. If he could have gotten out of prison he would have found Jamal and killed him. I don't know if he ever found him after he got out of jail. Probably not or we would have read about a murder in Tennessee, for real.

Now we were back with our deadbeat mom who, within days of our return was up to the same 'ol thing, doing drugs, selling drugs and neglecting us. She'd leave us with anyone who could look after us, even strangers. I was scared, especially after what had happened to us in Tennessee.

Having been kidnapped, I guess social services were more aware of us now. They made it clear to my mother that if she was going to take care of us she would have to clean up her act and stay drug free for a while. She tried to do it, but it did not last very long.

Pretty soon she was back on the streets. Then she saw my brother starting to sell drugs too. I guess she must have seen her life going backwards and realized that he was taking after her, so she took us to Social Services.

I remember her saying to me, “Momma’s gonna come right back and get you. They’re just going to take you in the back so you can write your name down and answer a few questions and stuff and I’ll be right back.” But she was gone. She left us in foster care. There were no goodbyes or anything.

My foster mom, Karyn

Karyn was a foster mother in the foster care system. She was, in one word, **EVIL**. My mom took my brother and I to the Social Services Center on Franklin Street in Brooklyn. She introduced us to one of the workers and told her that these were the kids she had been talking about. Apparently she had planned this out. She left us there and never returned.

After a little while, the social workers walked us to a car and told us they were going to take us for a ride. I wanted to wait until my mom returned but they told us that we should just go with them, so we did. We traveled to Jamaica Queens, where they parked the car and led us through a gate to a home that seemed to be in the back of a yard. A woman and two men were inside the modest house.

“Hello,” said the woman, who seemed to be quite cheerful and pleasant. My brother and I stood there staring, wondering who were these people? We waited for the two men to speak, but they said nothing. “This is Michael B. and Michael Jr.” The woman who introduced herself as Karyn explained. She was tall, had brown skin, and the thickest eyebrows I had ever seen. She was probably in her thirties at the time and when she spoke, she had a southern accent.

Michael B. was a very tall, dark-skinned man with a lot of facial hair. He also had the fattest stomach I had ever seen. I remember wondering how so much food could fit into one stomach. Then there was Michael Jr. who was also tall, with a slight beard and skinny legs. He was their son, probably around nineteen or twenty at the time.

While the social worker was there, Karyn showed off her house. She showed us where we would be sleeping, which seemed odd to me since I had no idea that we were going to be living there. But I didn’t say a thing. Then she proceeded to lead us to the kitchen where she had cooked for at least fifty people.

On the table was fried chicken, smothered chicken, pork chops, fish, white rice, collard greens, corn bread, macaroni and cheese, black-eyed peas, lima beans, cakes, pies. I mean this woman really won the social workers over with her presentation. Looking at all the food made me hungry. I also remember thinking that Karyn seemed like the nicest woman in the world. The social workers handed her an envelope and walked toward the door, "We'll call you soon," they said, and left.

When the door shut, I wanted to run for the door, grab on to the social worker's leg and beg her to take me back to my mother. But, I was afraid, so I just grabbed my brother's hand and started to cry. I knew this was the end, my mother was never coming back from that store and we would never ever see her again.

Before I could say or do anything, Karyn looked down at me and snapped loudly, **"STOP THAT CRYING NOW!"**

I quickly dried my eyes and fought back any more tears. Suddenly she seemed very scary. I was used to being yelled at by my mother and father, but to have this total stranger yell startled me. Michael Jr. took us upstairs to get us changed for dinner. But as I started to walk off with him, Karyn grabbed me by my arm and said quite menacingly, "There will be no crying around here!" Snatching my arm, I said, "You're not my mother. I want my mother."

She grabbed my cheeks really tight and said, "I'm your mother now and I don't plan to have any problems with you, you hear me?" I said nothing, **"DO YOU HEAR ME?"**

I said, "Yeah." "The word around here is **"YES!"** she responded. I swallowed hard, and said, "Yes." Then I followed my brother and Michael Jr. up the stairs.

From that day forward I would learn the true meaning of **EVIL, RELENTLESS, SELFISH**, and **CUNNING** and what a true **BITCH** was really like.

It was scary living with these people, especially after the nightmare of Tennessee. Once again, we were essentially living with total strangers. Apparently Karyn and Michael B. had somehow made it through the foster care screening process, or at least she did, and they were receiving $400 or $500 a month to spend on food, clothing and other necessities for us.

They were supposed to keep track of such spending and let social services know what the money was being spent on. I guess they must have lied, because most of the money went to buying beer for Karyn, who drank constantly. When we first got there, however, she did actually take us shopping for clothes and shoes. I guess that was to appease the social workers at the time because two years later I was still wearing the same clothes that were too small on me, and the same shoes that were hurting my feet.

It didn't take long before she graduated from yelling to physical abuse. Here we were, in a place in which we were supposed to be escaping the way our mother treated us but it was possibly even worse. Karyn thought nothing of backhanding me across the face or slapping me around while reminding me that she was in charge. Not that I really ever questioned her authority. If I didn't eat all of my food she would literally shove it in my mouth, close my jaw and make me try to eat it until I'd choke. It was horrifying.

When I wasn't in school I was usually cleaning the house for her and if I missed a spot she would hit me. And then of course my foster father began sexually abusing me. I say of course, because after Tennessee, nothing surprised me anymore. I couldn't tell Karyn anything about it or she'd beat me. She simply didn't care.

My brother was not going through the same treatment because most of the time he wasn't home. He had taken up a life of crime, hustling out on the streets, robbing, stealing, selling drugs and snatching pocketbooks. He was in and out of jail constantly. How the authorities never connected the fact that these people were supposed to be looking after him while he was always out on the streets getting into trouble was mindboggling.

What I found to be the worst thing of all was how my own mother turned a blind eye to all of this. Social services had a place in Queens where Karyn would bring us to sit with our mother for an hour or so. Surprisingly, she usually showed up. I'd tell her all the things that were going on.

Foster care service workers never knew about the abuse but here was my own mother listening to me telling her that I was being beaten by a psychotic woman and sexually abused by her deranged husband and she didn't seem concerned in the least. To her, this was better than having to take care of us. She'd always tell me that it was going to go away and that I should forget about it or try not to think about it. She wanted me to just sweep it all under the rug. I wanted her to tell social services so something could be done about the situation, but she never did.

After a few months, Karyn and Michael were actually allowed to take in more children. Social Services apparently thought I was doing just fine - they never asked me nor did they find out what was going on. So now, Karyn was getting more checks at about $400 or $500 per kid per month. There were two other young girls like myself who she started smacking around, backhanding across the face and force-feeding until they nearly choked. Then, just to show her "power" she'd make us all scrub the floors with toothbrushes. She must have learned this from some sadistic movie. I'm sure Michael was abusing them as well. Yes, Karyn and Michael were running their own little psychotic abuse camp and nobody ever knew it, except my own mom, who really didn't give a damn.

Looking Back

The situation was horrible and you may wonder why my hatred is more directed at Karyn than at Michael who sexually abused me. My feeling is that Karyn was completely in charge of everything and knew what was going on. I don't think Michael B ever wanted any kids there but he couldn't stand up to her. From what I saw, Michael B went to work and then went straight to his room, when he wasn't abusing me. I saw him as a sad and pathetic man, who showed fear when his wife was around. Even in his own home, this man had no balls. He only felt superior when he was raping a defenseless, underage child.

I believe he took out his sexual frustration on me because there were many times when Karyn would put him out of the room yelling, "Don't touch me…!" And then make him sleep on the couch in the living room next to his aging mother, who was also staying there much of the time.

There were plenty of times when they would argue about Karyn beer drinking, about money and his mother, whom Karyn also abused. She abused everyone in her path and in many ways he was a victim too. Their son Michael Jr. never touched me in any way shape or form. I rarely ever saw him and when I did, he always had a basketball in his hand or was with his girlfriend Carla. He may have known what was going on, but he wasn't about to get involved in his mother's business.

I felt betrayed by my own mother, who knew what was happening but just kept telling me to sweep it under the rug, never knowing what that meant and how hard that was for a child of abuse to do. I also felt let down by the system that had failed me because they never came to check on us.

They never talked to either of us, but instead only took Karyn's word over the phone about everything. They appreciated her because we were an emergency case and she took us right away, no questions asked. If they had asked some questions or checked on us I would have told them about the abuse and they would have seen me wearing the same old clothes Karyn had bought us when we first arrived. All of my dresses were at least three or four inches too short on me. Kids teased me at school about wearing the short dresses. Boys looked under my dress every chance they got. If my heels began to come off the bottom of my shoes I would use a hammer and nail to put them back together. No matter how much I cried and told my foster mom that I needed new clothes she just ignored me.

If they had come to check on us, the social workers could have also seen how tight the shoes were since my feet were still growing. You could see the corns on my feet and the soles of the shoes that were coming off. Those were signs of neglect that they would have noticed if they had gone out in the field to check on the situation in Karyn's house of horrors. Sad Realities of the Foster Care System

Yes, there are examples of kids who have made their way through the system without any traumatic stories, other than being separated from their birth parents. There are also stories of kids who have been adopted out of the foster care system into permanent loving homes. These are the positives.

Unfortunately, there are also many sobering statistics that come from the foster care system. Statistics show that individuals who were in foster care experience higher rates of physical and psychiatric morbidity than the general population. They also suffer from not being able to trust anyone, which can lead to permanent placements breaking down. In a study of adults who were in foster care in Oregon and Washington, they were found to have twice the incidence of depression (20 percent as compared to 10 percent) of people who never spent time in foster care. They also have a higher rate of post-traumatic stress disorder

(PTSD) than combat veterans. Children in foster care have a higher probability of having Attention Deficit Hyperactivity Disorder, deficits in executive functioning, increased anxiety, as well as other developmental problems. These children also experience higher degrees of incarceration, poverty, homelessness, and suicide.

Abuse and Negligence

Studies have indicated that abuse and neglect are more common in foster care situations than in the general population. This doesn't surprise me personally, especially since I had a friend living across the street from Karyn's home who had also been abused by her foster father. She, however, had a caring, non- abusive foster mom.

Studies from Johns Hopkins University here in the United States and from the United Kingdom both found that abuse and sexual abuse rates are much higher in foster care situations. In fact, the Johns Hopkins study had sexual abuse rates at four times higher in foster care situations and 28 times higher in group-homes than in the general population.

Some of the abuse cases have ended up in court where adults who were abused while in foster care when they were younger sued the foster parents. One of the most recent examples comes from California, where a man who had been placed in foster care in Santa Clara County sued for sexual damages that had occurred between 1995 and 1999. As it turned out, the foster parent was arrested and convicted in 2006 for nine counts of lewd or lascivious acts on a child by force, violence, duress, menace and fear. He was forcing children in his foster care to perform sex acts and as a result was sentenced to 220 years in prison.

Later that year, the foster family agency that licensed and was supposed to be monitoring the foster parent, was also found to be guilty for 75 percent of the abuse of the victim who was suing. The court awarded the victim $30 million dollars.

In Oregon, just three years ago, a horrifying story surfaced about twins who were kept in what were described as makeshift cages. Cribs covered by chicken wire were kept in what has been referred to as a dungeon, and the brother and sister went for long times without food or care. When they were adopted, their adoptive parents filed suit against the Oregon Department of Human Services and were awarded $2 million dollars to pay for the future care of the children.

Other lawsuits have been filed for sexual misconduct where young girls, much like myself, were the victims of such sexual abuse. It was found that a foster parent in Florida had been molester of children regularly for over sixteen years while a licensed foster parent. There were allegations of sexual misconduct for nearly a decade before he was finally arrested. Why nobody ever followed up on such allegations is a mystery.

There are good, well-meaning and caring people out there who serve as foster parents. Sadly, there are also those who are motivated by the money and are not fit to take on the responsibility of caring for children, such as Karyn. Screening of prospective foster parents must be much more intensive and follow-up visits are crucial. Those who are working in the system need to talk with the children and make sure everything is going well. Children can be very honest and know when they are being mistreated. Endangering children is a serious issue and people like my foster parents should not be able to slip through the system. We need to be able to place children away from deadbeat moms, in homes of trustworthy adults. Otherwise we are just taking kids from one abusive home to another.

CHAPTER 4

Stealing & Identity Theft

I'm not sure if many deadbeat moms have actually stolen their daughter's identity but it wouldn't surprise me one bit. I've heard of some moms using the fake birth certificates that used to come with Cabbage Patch dolls to claim more children on tax returns and other moms adding fictitious names to government forms in an attempt to get more funding. Using the real identity of one of your children wouldn't be that unusual for a deadbeat mom.

There was a very strange story from Wisconsin just a few years ago where a 33-year-old Green Bay woman claimed to be her 15-year-old daughter in order to make the high school cheerleading squad. Apparently her scheme worked and she made the squad, went to the pool parties, had a cheerleader's locker, attended practices and had a grand old time until someone caught on. The authorities took it quite seriously and charged her with identity theft, which is a felony. Her daughter was living with other family members in Nevada at the time so she didn't know anything about it until her mom was caught.

My story of identity theft, by my own mom, started when I was 18 and got married. It wasn't the smartest thing to do, but I wanted so badly to have something resembling a normal relationship. I'd met my husband, Rob, when we were both in the Job Corps in New York City. I was getting free job training to be a nurse's aide and he was training for a technology position. However, he decided that the Navy would be better for him than a civilian job so he enlisted shortly before we decided to get married. Then, shortly after we got married at the courthouse in downtown Manhattan, he was assigned for training at a naval base in South Carolina. So, we moved down there and we were set up in an apartment for military families near the base.

Other than my horrible experience in Nashville, I had never spent much time outside of New York City, so I immediately felt out of place. But I figured as long as we were together it would be okay and I'd get comfortable with the area, while spending time with my new husband. Boy was I wrong. Apparently Rob had neglected to tell me that he was heading out to sea. So, before I could finish unpacking he was gone. The next day I heard from him. He was already out at sea when he let me know that he was going to be away for three months. It was nice of him to give me a heads up. So there I was, on my own in South Carolina, in a furnished apartment on a naval base with nothing to do. I was used to working, which I had been doing since I was fifteen, so sitting around the house was new to me, and quite boring.

Rob told me that I didn't need to find a job because he would be getting his pay from the Navy. I spent most of my time pacing, watching television, pacing some more and wondering what I was going to do to keep from going crazy. He had told me not to get too familiar with the other wives since a lot of them slept around, had threesomes and did all sorts of weird things. At the time I didn't even know what he was talking about. I remember thinking to myself "threesomes?" Then one day I took a walk with one of the other wives and I remember her meeting up with some guy. Pretty soon I caught on to the idea of what Rob was talking about from our conversations so I excused myself and continued spending most of my time alone.

Finally after three boring months my husband was home and I thought things would change and we would spend time together. Wrong again! After one month he was gone and once again I didn't even know where he went. There I was, asking people on the base where he was until finally his Sergeant sent him a note asking him why he kept going out to sea without telling his wife He added that it wasn't right. Once again I heard from Rob, who told me that he was sorry and that he meant to tell me that he was going away again. I don't understand how you can get married and forget to tell your wife that you'll be out at sea for nine months. So, I explained to him that I had done the three months, but I was not going to hang around the Navy base for another nine. I'd heard about crimes and violence in various parts of South Carolina and didn't really want to stay there by myself. Plus there really wasn't much of anything for me to do.

So I headed back to New York, moved in with my dad and started doing some volunteer work at a hospital in hopes of getting hired. Meanwhile, Rob's superiors had made sure that he had filled out the paper work for me to receive some of his pay every month. Rob set it up so that he would have my checks sent to New York. Since I didn't know exactly where I was going to be living, not really wanting to stay too long at my father's house with him watching my every move, I had the checks sent to my mother's address. She was now living with her lady friend, Charlotte, and Charlotte's family in the Bronx. I explained that the checks would be sent to her and she told me it would be no problem. They would each be for $800.

The first check was sent out on schedule. As a result, I decided to move out of my father's home but not before I asked him for a small loan, because I knew my allotment was on the way. I took the money he loaned me and got myself a room, some food, and some new clothes. I had also started looking for work even though I was receiving the military checks. I had no luck finding work so I really needed that money to take care of the bills.

"Your check is here is what I heard my mother say when she called me".

When I arrived at my mother's house to pick up the check, she told me she had made a mistake, my check had not come. She thought it was in the mailbox but it was something else. So I called the Navy immediately and told them that the check was overdue for delivery. I was told to give them a number where they could reach me and they explained that they would check on the money. About an hour later I received a call from them telling me that the check was sent out on September 5th.

It was now September 19th, so I asked them to put a stop on the check because it must have gotten lost. So they did, and I was told that they would send a replacement check in a week.

A week later I received the copy of the check I thought was lost, it had been already signed and cashed, I was told that I had to first sign papers stating that it was not my signature and if I recognized the handwriting, I should let them know whose it was. I did not know who had signed the check and I wrote back telling them so. By the end of September I had finally received a replacement check and I was relieved because my bills were overdue.

The following month, on October 10th I made a trip to The Bronx looking for the next check. Once again, when I got there my mom told me that there was no check. The next day she said no check, every day for the next couple of weeks, "no check". Once again I called the Navy and they told me that the checks were being delivered to the given address and the occupants in the apartment were under investigation. I never told my mother what they had told me, but now I knew something was wrong.

Now I was confused, upset and broke. The landlord for the room I was renting was getting tired of me paying late, and was threatening to kick me out. I had to go to the one person I suspected was cashing my checks and stealing my money, my own mother. I had called her before I went over there to let her know I needed a loan to pay my bills.

When I got there I just started crying because I could not believe she could be that person who would take her own daughter's money. She slapped me in my face and told me to shut the f--k up with all that crying. I was so angry I began to walk away but she grabbed me again and once more told me to shut the f--k up. So I stopped crying and she said, "Okay, you want some money now come on?"

I followed her down the stairs as she headed toward the check-cashing store. Now I was thinking that perhaps she tried to cash it and they told her to get me. So I went in with hopes of seeing if maybe my check was sitting there waiting for me. When I got there my mother introduced me to the lady working at the check-cashing store. She gave me some paper to sign. I signed it thinking she was about to give me my check and instead she handed me about $200.00 in fake money.

I looked at her and asked, "What's this?" She told me it was the food stamps that I had just signed up for. Before I could respond, my mother grabbed me and she pushed me out of the door. I said, "Ma, I didn't apply for food stamps! Why did you go to public assistance and use my name for food stamps?" She did not answer. Instead she grabbed half of the stamps and walked away. Before she walked off I gave her a look of shock and disbelief. She told me that if I looked at her again like that, she would slap me down to the ground. Then she said, "Now I'm not giving you any money for your rent." This was no big surprise considering she never gave me anything,

As she walked, she kind of shoved me with her shoulder and I pushed back. She went to hit me and I grabbed her arm and shoved it. I warned her if she put her hand on me again, as much as I didn't want to do it, I would hit her back. She looked at me, not sure if I was serious, but willing to find out. At that moment one of her friends stepped in and separated us.

I walked away, and got on the bus heading back to Harlem. I realize now that not only had this person stolen my checks, she had also stolen my identity. I didn't return to my mother's house for a very long time after that. It was a lucky thing that I found a job right before being evicted, and I was able to pay some rent. My husband helped me out with some money out of pocket. This allowed me to open a bank account and soon I was able to have the checks he sent me go straight into the bank. I didn't tell the Navy about my mom, but my husband may have because they went after her to get their money back. I guess she paid them back. She didn't want to go back to jail; the Navy is like the IRS. They won't let up until they get what they want.

I guess somehow it was settled so I didn't bother to ask. I think I was still shocked that my own mother would steal my money. Somehow, I always gave her the benefit of the doubt. I guess I always thought she'd change, but deadbeat moms rarely do—unless you can get through to them.

Over the next ten years she managed to use my name to get jobs and make money. She looked young for her age but not in her twenties, which is how old I was at the time. Yet, somehow she did not get caught. She worked in a clothing store for kids and then at some other jobs.

The fact that we were going by the same name no longer affected me because there was nothing else she could take from me. During these years I was receiving the checks directly from my husband that she couldn't go after. She was smart enough to get a different social security number while still using my background information as hers. I assume that her friend Charlotte taught her a lot of this stuff, from forgery to getting a fake social security number, since I don't think my mom could figure all this out by herself. I recently learned that to this day she is still using my name, on her utility bills.

As for my husband, even though he and I were going through our own problems, largely because we were living apart most of the time, he still helped take care of me financially, even when I was working. He visited me often in New York, which was fine for a while, but eventually it all fell apart and we got divorced.

After several jobs in hospitals and elsewhere I got a job at the Long Island Railroad (LIRR) and in time I even began to forgive my mother, yet again. I even encouraged her to work for the LIRR but only under her real name. Otherwise I was afraid that one of us, or both of us, would get arrested for fraud, since she was still using my background information to go with her fake social security number. Eventually she applied under her real name. Somehow, despite her criminal record, she was able to get an entry-level job cleaning stations. I guess they believed in second chances, I guess I did too. Many other people would have stopped having anything to do with her years ago after all she had done, stealing my name and identity, not to mention all that she had put me through earlier in my life.

My Daughter and my Mom

While she did take my money and my identity, one thing my mother could not take from me was my daughter, the love of my life. One of the toughest things about having a deadbeat mom (or dad) in your life is that eventually you will have a child and they will ask about their grandma, or grandpa. Her grandfather, my dad, had died by the time she was born – something my mom didn't tell me, another thorn in our relationship. My dad had gotten sick in June of 1993.

My aunt (my father's sister) told my mom to let me know that he was very ill but my mom didn't tell me anything. The doctor had told them that he might not make it until the end of the year.

I was having a difficult pregnancy and the doctors were worried that I could lose my baby. So, at the time he passed away, I was in the hospital. My mother and brother knew I was there but neither one told me. It was my aunt who finally told me that he died and that was several weeks later. I will never forgive my mom for that. My aunt still does not speak to me. She asked me how I could not come to my own father's funeral. I told her I was in the hospital and no one told me.

To this day I don't think my aunt believes that my mother did not tell me. She also doesn't know how much my mother hated him and how she couldn't accept that I didn't hate him, and that we actually got along.

Nonetheless, I decided that I would let my daughter have some kind of relationship with my mother. In the hopes that after all these years, my mom had changed. After all, she was now more responsible and an actual part of Charlotte's family.

It seemed that Charlotte really wanted my daughter around, since her own grown daughter had two young children.

Unlike my mom, Charlotte and her daughter were pretty good at taking care of their kids, so I began to feel comfortable letting my daughter visit and spend some time with them in the Bronx where they were all living.

The kids would play and everyone seemed to get along fairly well. My mother was not very involved, which was typical of her. However, she didn't seem to be strung out on drugs either, which was a good sign. If the kids misbehaved, as young children often do, Charlotte and her daughter would discipline them by giving them a time out.

It seemed that all was peaceful for a while until one day Charlotte pulled me aside and told me that on a few occasions when my mom was watching the kids, she would beat my daughter if she misbehaved.

According to Charlotte, this was not just a spanking, but my mom would start beating her so badly that when she heard the crying she would run in and have to physically separate them. This would lead to major fights between Charlotte and my mother. Apparently, Charlotte, who had done time in jail, was still more adept at raising and taking care of children than my mom, whose answer to anything was still hitting, beating and abuse.

I approached my mother and told her what Charlotte had said to me and I explained that this was MY daughter and that she was NOT to strike her ever again. She agreed, but I still did not feel comfortable letting my daughter see her for long periods of time. Eventually, some of the other neighborhood children with whom my daughter had played in the Bronx began asking what had happened to her. They wanted to play with her again. By now she was about seven, so I let her play with them on occasion.

Unfortunately children learn from the abuse they see around them. One afternoon she was playing house with another child. My daughter was posing as the child and the other girl, around the same age, was playing the mom. I'm not sure exactly what happened, but the other girl started to beat my daughter so hard that she had black and blue marks all over her backside. That was the last straw for me. It seemed to me that nobody was paying attention to these kids. After this incident she would no longer return to the Bronx.

From that time on, my mom only saw my daughter with me around and in my home, or at least in our neighborhood.

Some Things Never Change

Clearly having a mom who would steal your money and identity can cause you to be distrustful. Yet, I never wanted to completely give up on her and always tried to have some contact with her, hoping she could change, despite all that she had done over the years. Perhaps I'm an eternal optimist. One night when my daughter was playing with her dolls, she began to play rough, hitting them, throwing them around, and claiming that they were not behaving. I asked her why was she treating her dolls like that, she said that is how her grandmother had treated her. Once when they went to Popeye's Chicken her grandmother had grabbed her by the collar and had threatened to completely throw her through the glass window if she didn't behave. Then I asked, her "How did that make you feel?"

She said she didn't know, so I asked her if she could draw me a picture of how that made her feel. She started to draw monsters and very ugly images. I also noticed that it was around that time that she stopped looking out the window which she liked to do with her dolls in the morning. Her sleeping pattern also changed and she had begun to climb into bed with me, sleeping with one of her feet pushed against me.

I found a child psychologist at a local hospital. After some time spent with my daughter, the therapist showed me some more pictures that my daughter had drawn. They were angry and violent. She also gave me a report on my daughter whom she felt had been abused by my mom.

I was to keep her away from my mom or she would have to report both of us to social services. I met up with my mother and told her she could no longer visit my home or my daughter.

My mother and I had no contact for years. She would call every now and then to say she was sorry and never meant to hurt my daughter. She would cry on the phone and hang up. After a few years of therapy, my daughter's behavior was slowly changing back to normal. She didn't see her grandmother again until she was fourteen years old and even then I would not let her stay with her without me being around.

My daughter is now nineteen and she rarely ever sees her grandmother though they do talk on the phone. My mom will tell her that she will buy her things or do things for her that she never does. I can't believe she's still doing that – it's the same thing she did with me, and my brother. Nothing has changed. I tell my daughter to simply ignore what her grandmother tells her so she won't be disappointed like I was. She doesn't completely understand, but she's learning that there are some people you simply cannot trust and her grandmother is one of those people.

The story of my deadbeat mom is both similar and different from many others. It's similar in that it's a story of ongoing neglect and abuse, not to mention distrust. It’s different in that many deadbeat mom stories end with a complete split in the relationship in which the child gives up on their mom

I guess I could never quite give up hope that things would be different.

I hoped that she could perhaps right some of her wrongs by being better with her granddaughter. She had a second chance, but she blew it. Perhaps I should have known better. I’ve tried very hard to raise my daughter in a completely different manner than I was raised. That’s why when I learned that my mom was abusing her it hurt me so deeply. It was exactly what I did not want to happen. I was too trusting.

Now I tell other people that if they have grown up with a deadbeat mom who was neglectful, abusive and/or dishonest, never to give them the benefit of the doubt. It’s too easy for people to say they’ve changed. They need to show you that they have realized the errors of their ways. Unless you've witnessed such a change first-hand and they have opened up to you and let you know that they are aware of what they did wrong, they may not have changed at all. That’s why it’s so important to get deadbeat moms to understand the effects of their actions on others, even on their grandchildren. It's also important to recognize when no such change has occurred so you can keep your child or children safe from them.

CHAPTER 5

THE NEGLECTFUL PARTY GIRL

There comes a time in life when you need to accept responsibility for yourself and for someone else. When the doctor placed my daughter in my arms for the first time, I knew that she was my number one concern and that my days of late night partying were over. Yet some moms apparently never learn.

Tanya is a single mom who moved into the building where I was living with my daughter. One day we met while entering the building. She held the door for me while I brought in my groceries.

I lived on the second floor and she lived on the first floor of the walk-up apartment building. I was one of the youngest tenants there along with Tanya, whom I think is a couple years older than I am.

She was a black woman with a medium light complexion and she reminded me of a friend I had who always loved to be out at the bars or clubs, drank a lot and had lots of male friends. We called her a party girl, not unlike Tanya. We never really became friends but Tanya and I exchanged greetings whenever we saw each other coming and going. Her son, Tyrone, was about the same age as my daughter and they would play together in front of the building along with other kids from the neighborhood. Some of us parents would sit nearby and keep an eye on them while they played. Others, like me, would watch from our windows. Tanya was almost never one of those parents. It wasn't long after she moved in that I could hear a number of men coming and going from Tanya's apartment, which was right below mine. I would also hear them honking their horns from out front, with loud music booming from their car stereos interrupted by the driver yelling to Tanya to hurry up, as it was "time to party." I would look out the window with my daughter and we would often see Tanya getting into a car with some guy and heading out for the evening. When she was home, there would be friends coming up to visit her and many parties at her house.

Meeting Tyrone

Whenever I would call my daughter in for lunch or supper, she would often bring one or two of her friends in with her. I never thought twice about feeding her friends. Tyrone would often be one of the kids who came in to eat. I had no problem with him eating at my house, he seemed like a nice boy, but I wanted to know that it was okay with his mom. I knew the mom of my daughter's other friends and she was fine with her kids coming by to eat at my house.

When she first brought Tyrone over, I had only seen him from out my window so I asked my daughter, "Who is this nice little boy?" She told me that his name was Tyrone, so I asked where he was from and whether his parents knew he was here. She just shrugged her shoulders and sat down at the table with the kids to eat.

Later I asked her again about Tyrone and she told me that his mother was downstairs and her name was Tanya. Until that point I had no idea that Tanya had children, since I never saw her with them. I then put two and two together and realized that party girl had a child whom she was barely seen with and most likely was improperly taking care of.

Unlike most of the kids who would ask their moms if they could come over, he never seemed to ask Tanya, who was rarely ever around. For days Tyrone would come up and eat dinner with my daughter even when the other kids went home to eat. The way he ate so quickly gave me the impression that he didn't eat often enough. Sometimes I would have to tell him to slow down because I was worried that he would choke. He was frail, yet when I fed him, he loved to eat. In some ways he reminded me of myself as a child, frail, and eating everything very fast. When you go for long stretches without food, you tend to get excited when it's on the table in front of you and start gobbling it down. After dinner I would walk him downstairs to his apartment. Once I told him that I'd like to say hi to his mom. He told me that she wasn't there very often, which I sort of knew from seeing her take off in cars with guys all the time.

When we'd get to his door, I'd make sure he went inside and locked the door. I would ask him if he was scared to be in the house by himself. He said no. He seemed to be a slightly slow thinker from the way he responded to questions. He walked on his tippy toes and one of his hands hung down as if he had no control over it.

Once, when I walked Tyrone to the door I asked him if he ate breakfast. He explained that he could not touch food or feed himself until his mom gave him permission. I told him if he ever got hungry and his mom wasn't there he could come upstairs and eat breakfast with my daughter. He said, "Okay." Then he went in the house and locked the door behind him.

At one point Tyrone mentioned that he hardly ever saw his dad but that he had a sister. Since I never saw his sister I assumed she must have been living with the dad or with her grandparents. Then, a couple of years later, she was suddenly on the scene, living with Tyrone and his mom. Her name was Shameeka, and she was about two years younger than Tyrone and my daughter.

I met Shameeka the same way I met my daughter's other friends, at my kitchen table. I asked my daughter, "Who is this pretty little girl?" My daughter responded that this was Tyrone's sister. She was shy, but not frail, and didn't gobble down her food like her brother, so I knew that wherever she had been, they had been taking care of her. I waved at her and she waved back.

From that day forward, my daughter began playing with Shameeka a lot in our apartment. Whenever dinner was ready I set out two plates for my daughter and Shameeka, plus one more for Tyrone. By that point, Tyrone kind of knew when dinner was ready so he just knocked on the door and I let him in. After dinner he would take his sister downstairs, telling me that his mother wanted him to bring her home after they ate. While she never said anything to me, I knew at least that Tanya was aware that her kids were eating at my house. Shortly after meeting Shameeka, I met her father while passing in the lobby of our building. He was a tall brown skinned male standing about six feet tall.

He was carrying some of Shameeka's belongings and after saying hello; he mentioned that his daughter was going off to stay with him for a week. He seemed to pay attention to her and treat her well, so I assumed that this was who she had been with all those years before my daughter and I met her. Early one morning, a week later, when her father brought Shameeka home, I heard him and Tanya arguing about leaving the kids in the house by themselves while she partied all night. They argued often but this time it was loud enough so I could hear what was going on. He threatened to take Shameeka from her and contact social services if she did not change. But his words apparently fell on deaf ears as Tanya continued to leave her children alone at all hours while she took in the New York club scene.

Then one Saturday night, about a month after Shameeka had moved in, there was a knock on my door at about 7 pm. It was Tanya. She asked if I could babysit Shameeka for an hour, which I agreed to. I had watched Shameeka a couple of times before and knew she would be no problem. When I asked where Tyrone was, she told me he had already gone to sleep. Shameeka came in and played with my daughter.

Well, eight o'clock came and went. As did nine o'clock, and still Tanya was a no-show. She had given me a number where she could be reached, but when I called the number, it was not in service. I began to worry.

I put Shameeka in a pair of my daughter's pajamas, fed her dinner and put her to bed. At about ten o'clock the following morning there was a knock at the door. It was Tanya, with several apologies about how she fell asleep at her friend's house and this situation would never happen again.

Two days later at about eight o'clock in the evening, Tyrone knocked on the door and asked if he and his sister could have something to eat and drink. I could never deny children food, but first I asked him where his mother was. He responded that she hadn't come home since last night and there was no food in the house. I invited both children in for a hot meal and a cold drink. As I saw Shameeka and Tyrone standing at my door I saw my brother and myself as young children, left alone and hungry, knocking on Katrina's door. They ate dinner and I invited them to stay until their mother got back. But Tyrone said they were supposed to stay at home and that he would look after his little sister. I walked them to their apartment and once again made sure they were inside and the door was locked. Tanya continued staying out late and partying on a regular basis. Her kids were over frequently. Nights would come and go and Tanya was nowhere to be found. They would go home and stay alone. It bothered me because I knew exactly what they were going through.

One night, at about 2 am, I was awakened by Shameeka yelling, "Stop." My apartment was right over theirs, but that's how loud she was yelling. I had walked them down earlier and I know they locked their door so I was pretty sure nobody else was in the apartment but her and her brother. When she yelled his name and told him to stop touching her, I knew what was going on. I banged on the radiator that was one of those poll radiators that went from floor to floor, and apparently they heard me. After that everything was quiet. The next night Tyrone did not come up for dinner. My plan was not to say anything to him, but wait and see if it happened again. The following night I heard her yelling the same thing. Now it was really beginning to bother me, so I went downstairs and banged on the door. I shouted for him to leave her alone. Once again things got quiet and stayed that way. Tyrone waited about three days before bothering his sister again. Then, like before, I heard Shameeka yelling for her brother to stop. Again, I went to their door and knocked hard telling Tyrone to stay away from her.

Finally, I decided it was time to talk to Tanya about what was going on. I didn't really want to do it, and didn't know how she was going to take such news but I thought she should be aware and deal with her son. So on a Saturday morning I knocked on Tanya's door with Shameeka by my side and I told Shameeka to tell her mother what her brother had been doing to her.

She told her mother that he had been touching her and pointed to where. I told Tanya of the previous incidents where I had knocked on the door or radiator warning Tyrone to stop. Since he would not stop, I thought it would be better to bring it to her attention.

Tanya calmly thanked me, then grabbed her daughter and pulled her into the house. In an instant the door was closed and I could hear the screaming as she started beating Shameeka. I stood their frozen, not knowing what to do. I heard Tanya yelling, "Why didn't you come to me, "You know your brother is retarded!" All I could do was cry. It was my fault. I wanted to go and stop it but I didn't want to get Shameeka into more trouble and be seriously hurt, nor did I want to end up fighting with Tanya. For the next couple of weeks I did not see Shameeka, nor did Tyrone come upstairs for dinner. I was worried about them, especially Shameeka.

After about three weeks I heard Shameeka's father banging on the door downstairs. He was yelling from outside the door at Tanya. Telling her that he was going to kill her, and that retarded son of hers.

"You let the Mother-f---er touch my daughter? I knew this would happen! You are never home!"

This went on for a few minutes until he finally left, yelling that he would see her since he knew the clubs she hung out at every night. He also added that he would call social services on her. Later that day, I saw Tanya and Tyrone getting into a taxi with a couple of suitcases. I thought that this might mean they were leaving and Shameeka was now with her dad. A couple of months later, however, Tyrone was back outside playing with the other kids and Tanya was still running out every night to party. Apparently some things never change.

I told my daughter to stay away from him and explained that he likes to touch girls and that she should not let any one touch her. I still let him come to the house to eat, but made him sit with other boys. I was troubled by what he had been doing to his sister but I could not deny him food. If there were no other boys for him to sit with,

I would wrap up some food for him and walk him back downstairs to his apartment to eat it, again making sure he closed and locked the door behind him.

I saw Shameeka occasionally when she visited her mom and brother. Years passed by and I started to see Shameeka in the streets, she started hanging out with a group of "fast" girls who were spending a lot of time with some of the local boys. I'm sure many of them were becoming sexually active at an early age. Today, Shameeka and Tyrone say hi and they are friendly to my daughter, although they don't hang out together. As for Tanya, she's gotten older, as we all do, but she still takes some time to go out and party. She doesn't pay much attention to what her kids are up to, but she never really did. And, she still never thanked me for all the meals I gave them while she was out painting the town or for letting her know that her daughter was being abused. As I said earlier, some things never change.

Can't Stop Partying

There are many adults who can't quite accept that it's time to grow up, take responsibility and stop the partying. Fortunately, some are able to juggle the party lifestyle by night, and be there to take care of their kids by day. Others have parents, relatives or friends to help raise their kids. I helped Tanya by feeding her kids, but not by raising them. It wasn't my place.

I've seen similar problems to Tanya's, with other women in my neighborhood, partying at all hours and leaving their kids to fend for themselves. I knew this scenario as a child very well. Children should not be left to raise themselves. It makes them fearful of adults and often they seek the attention they are not getting from their parents, from other people, often the wrong people. I experienced some bad relationships when I started dating because I was seeking the attention I never got at home. But unlike the party moms, I changed my lifestyle when my daughter was born—not that I was ever that much of a party girl. I saw my daughter as a marvelous reason to change my life so I could be there for her.

Party girls like Tanya are not maternal and simply see children as obstacles in the way of having a good time. After all, it's all about them. Interestingly enough, Shameeka's dad could see that in Tanya and recognized that he needed to get his daughter away from her.

I don't know if Shameeka's father ever called social services on Tanya, although she did stop running around so much. I felt responsible for Shameeka being beaten by Tanya. I was glad, however, that she told her father and that rather than taking it out on her, he came to get her to live with him.

As for Tyrone his father is out of the picture making it that much worse for him because he have no other adult to intervene.

It was also from the situation with Tanya that I realized how easy it was for me to recognize a neglected child. I knew Tyrone was neglected from the first time I saw him. Unlike physical abuse, where the signs are often more visible, signs of neglect are a little more subtle. Even so social services reports that instances of neglect are just as high as reports of physical violence. Unlike physical violence which typically occurs when the parent is angry, frustrated or under the effects of drugs or alcohol, neglect is usually ongoing in the child's life.

Here are some of the signs I saw in Tyrone, who was clearly a victim of a neglectful deadbeat mother:

- A frail appearance. This showed he was underfed.
- The fast and furious way in which he ate also indicated that he was not being fed on a regular basis.
- His dirty ears and hair indicated that his hygiene was not being looked after.

- His clothes, that didn't match and were often not warm enough for the weather, indicated he was dressing himself.
- The fact that I would sometimes see him during the school day, meaning nobody was making him go to school.

What was interesting about Tanya was that when Shameeka arrived, she suddenly felt the need to ask me to babysit. Unlike Tyrone, whom she had never asked me to watch; she took some responsibility for Shameeka. I figured out later that she was on a short leash when it came to shared-custody of her daughter.

Unlike Tyrone's farther who had disappeared from the picture, Shameeka's dad was very much in the picture and agreed only to let her share custody if she was responsible. She wanted to show that she was doing the right thing by having a sitter watch the children when she went out. But after a while she couldn't even bother arranging for me, or someone else, to watch them so she left Shameeka alone with Tyrone. At the time, he was about ten and she was about eight.

In the end, it cost her. Shameeka's dad took her away from Tanya when he found out that Tyrone had been touching her inappropriately. It's hard for someone who is, by nature, neglectful, to suddenly take on responsibility, and Tanya couldn't handle it. The good thing was that Shameeka's father probably gave her a better life. While she was living with him, I did see her occasionally and she never appeared frail, neglected or abused. I have no idea what her home life was like, but it appeared that she was better off with her dad.

What's kind of sad about the deadbeat party mom is that she is typically seeking something "wonderful" in her life when she already has that—a child. There are so many young women, myself included, who look forward to being a mom that it is hard to see women like Tanya who do not appreciate it or rise to the occasion.

Blunt Moms

Along with party moms there are also what we call blunt moms. They are essentially moms who party and smoke pot with their kids. It extends to trying too hard to be cool with the kids rather than drawing the line between what is acceptable and what is not as a parent. Here are a few examples from such moms that I know.

1. Brittany is a young girl from the neighborhood who has a blunt mom. Her mom sits home all day, does basically nothing and collects food stamps. Brittany's mom lets her and her two other sisters have boys spend the night with them, and allows them to curse, smoke and drink. Brittany's oldest sister got pregnant at 17. The mom knew but didn't really care; she just helped her with the baby. The mom smokes weed with 15 year-old Brittany almost every day if she wants to. When she wants to smoke she simply asks her kids' and friends. 'Who's going to light it up?' She doesn't think it's bad for her kids and actually thinks it will make them closer. Brittany stays home from school when she wants and her mom doesn't really say anything. She allows the kids to do whatever they wanted because she thinks it's cool.

2. Grant's mom is also unemployed and living off of public assistance with six teenagers and six grandchildren. She has so many children that she lets them do anything they want. They smoke, drink alcohol, watch sex movies on television and spend the night out whenever they want. When she tried parenting it didn't work because they didn't listen, so she gave up and simply tried to "fit in." Now, when her older kids bring their friends over she joins them and smokes weed. The kids label their mom as "cool" but we all know that's just not the case. She tries being her kid's friend more than being a responsible mom leaving her kids with no boundaries.

3. Cindy is a new blunt mom. She is 28 and still living with her mother. She just had a newborn baby whom she smokes blunts all day around. The baby's father is a marijuana dealer on the streets and the Cindy lets him stay with them because he's her supplier. Cindy thinks nothing of smoking weed around the baby and Cindy's mother doesn't seem to care. In fact, they have blunt parties with plenty of the local kids and their moms, smoking and drinking around them.

4. Samantha, who is seventeen, has a mom that allows her to drink alcohol. She has already learned how to make all sorts of drinks, thanks to her mom who works as a bartender. Once, when I was at her house with some other friends, Samantha offered drinks to her mom and I. Samantha and her mother drank and talked as if they were good old drinking buddies. I like the fact that her mother is cool, but not in that way. Some parents will be lenient on their children when it comes to smoking and drinking, but to encourage it and make it a regular routine is not beneficial to Samantha. I hope Samantha does not grow up to be an alcoholic… I lost a friend that way.

Blunt moms are dangerous in the examples that they set and their inability to recognize what is and is not appropriate behavior. Sure some of us like to stretch the boundaries a little and it's great to have a positive relationship with your kids, even being "friends" to some degree. But there still needs to be some amount of parenting and responsibility.

Chapter 6

Having a Child to Keep a Man

The idea that a baby will keep a couple together is not at all new. Couples have used this as a means of trying to save a bad relationship or a failing marriage for many years. Typically it doesn't work. Most often having a baby to care for does not solve the problem.

The other issue is the child is not at fault for the couple's inability to stay together, yet he or she often suffers the consequences of such an ill-advised plan. Too often, the mom simply does not understand that the child still needs the love and attention even after the marriage or relationship is over.

My brother's girlfriend, Janine, was a mom who decided to have a baby to keep her rocky relationship together. In the end it was the child who really suffered.

When the relationship started, my brother and Janine seemed to be a happy couple, doing everything together and even dressing alike when they went out on the town. There wasn't anything Janine would not do to please him. When she told everyone she was pregnant, our family and friends were all happy for her and for my brother. She seemed to be so in love with him and told everybody that he was the one. After their daughter Ruby was born, my brother took on several jobs all at one time to make sure both Janine and Ruby had everything. He worked hard and was happy to see that his family was doing well.

This, however, only lasted a few months. As time went on, work began to slow down and money became tight. He continued to find whatever he could, but without any formal education or training, he was limited to specific jobs. As the money got tighter, the arguments began. My brother, who was used to going without very much, didn't know what to do to keep Janine happy. After some time, he resorted to selling drugs on the streets, something he had learned from our mother. This solved their money problems for a short time, until he got arrested and ended up in jail for several months.

Once he was out of jail and back home with Janine and Ruby, the fighting resumed and the relationship deteriorated quickly. So did Janine's parenting. Apparently she only had Ruby to make the relationship work. When it didn't, she essentially cast her own daughter aside and went out with other men.

The problem was that her daughter was not disposable and needed a mom. Janine completely neglected Ruby. It got to the point where social services attempted to take Ruby away from her, but Janine would cry and promise to be a better parent. For some reason, even with evidence to the contrary, social services let Janine maintain custody of her daughter. This scenario played out time after time. And, every time social services let her keep her daughter, she would turn around and do the same thing, neglect her. Not that I'm a savior or anything like that, but I couldn't stand seeing Ruby like this and I begged her to let me take Ruby in for a while, which she did.

I remember bringing her to my house in a stroller. She was four years old and not even walking yet. It was heartbreaking to see her like this. I tried to talk Janine into letting me adopt her. She went back and forth, at some points thinking it might be a good idea and then changing her mind. Meanwhile, Ruby was living with me, and I had a seven year-old daughter at the time. Every time it seemed that Janine was going to come and take her home, my daughter and I would pack up her stuff and prepare. Then Janine would call and tell us that she wasn't coming so we'd unpack. After doing this a few times I figured we'd just pack up her stuff if and when Janine showed up.

Janine was living on welfare, so she didn't want social services to know Ruby was living with me. She was getting more money because of Ruby, not that she was giving me any of it for taking care of her. I too was getting financial assistance while going to school for computer processing. I was also spending some of my money on Ruby. There was a neighbor and friend of mine across the street who was able to take in the girls for a little while so I could go to school, as well as later on when I got temp jobs. I gave her some money for helping me out

Meanwhile, as Ruby stayed with me, Janine confessed to me that she had found a new way of making money, prostitution. The problem was that she wasn't a very good businesswoman. She was letting men have anal sex with her for $5! It was bad enough she had to resort to prostitution, but for five bucks? Really? Anyway, assuming she was probably in pain much of the time, I reassured her that I would keep Ruby with me for as long as she liked.

One thing I immediately noticed when Ruby tried to walk was that she could not manage to get her left leg to follow her right leg. It dragged when she would get up and, as a result, she could not walk. Janine had kept her in the stroller or lying down for over four years so the leg had no strength. Her other leg was stronger, but also wobbly. I also noticed when I went to change her clothes that she was still in pampers. When I'd ask her what she wanted to eat she'd just say, "Hmm..." Then point to something. Ruby could not speak either.

I started by getting her to take small steps so she would feel comfortable. Each day my daughter and I would help her walk a little more and we'd hold onto her. Ruby's one leg was like a rubber band. I didn't really understand it, but we kept taking steps with her and slowly the leg got stronger day by day. I was relieved that no long lasting damage had been done to her leg. Finally, after a few months, Ruby was running around all over the place.

I also started asking her what foods she wanted and when she'd point to something, I'd say the name of the food a few times until she would repeat it. Even if she couldn't name it, I'd feed her so she wouldn't starve. But, little by little, she began talking. I also taught her how to use the bathroom. It amazed me that Janine had never taught her to do anything.

Finally, once Ruby was walking and talking, I arranged for her to go to a wonderful summer program called Camp Getaway, with Janine's okay. I knew the lady who ran it and my daughter had gone there when she was younger. Ruby liked it a lot. It was the first time she ever really got to run around with other kids her age. The woman who ran it took a liking to Ruby. I told her a little about Ruby being behind in her development, and she took great care of her. When it was getting close to the end of the summer, Ruby made it clear that she did not want to leave and the woman who ran the camp, now understanding more about Ruby's home life from some of our conversations, wanted to keep Ruby. She talked to Janine about the possibility of becoming Ruby's legal guardian, and brought me along to explain how well this could work for all concerned. At first Janine thought it might be a good idea, but soon her attitude changed and she began writing threatening letters to the woman at Camp Getaway accusing her of trying to steal her child. At that point I explained to both sides that this was probably not a good idea.

Janine also wanted Ruby to come home a week early and was rather insistent, so I brought her back early with clothes and toys that the woman at the camp had given her. Janine didn't let Ruby have very much of this stuff and stored some of it at my house. Ruby, however, had developed a love of art and if you asked her what she wanted for Christmas, she would say an easel and crayons or other art supplies.

It didn't take long before Ruby was living with me again. Janine was back to her neglectful, deadbeat self and Ruby was once again a "burden to her". I found this to be quite upsetting because she was a good kid and very easy to take care of. I introduced her to macaroni and cheese and she was thrilled. She'd eat dinner and go in her room and start coloring. Ruby did not ask for much of anything and was happy with simple things.

After a while, it became evident that someone was going to have to enroll her in school and I pretty much knew that would have to be me. I called Janine who had not done anything about signing Ruby up for school. The school year had begun but since Janine was living in the South Bronx, I don't think anyone knew or cared that she had a daughter who wasn't attending school. I told Janine that I would enroll her in the school near my house, where my daughter was going, and when she was ready to take her back, she could transfer her to the local school near her home.

I started her off in Kindergarten. The term began and ended and Ruby was still with me. First grade came and went and Janine still did not take Ruby back. It was finally after the second grade that Janine was ready to resume her role as "parent," and I use the term quite loosely. Janine wanted her daughter back because my brother, who had spent the last couple of years in jail for selling drugs, again, was coming home. This was her chance to once again have a family life with her daughter and my brother living happily under one roof. At least that was what she envisioned.

My brother would call from prison whenever he had the opportunity and wondered where Ruby was. For a long time

Janine would tell him that she was playing or sleeping or something. But since this had gone on for more than two years, he became wise to the fact that something was strange. He wanted to talk to his daughter. So, she just started responding to his questions about Ruby with, "Ask your sister." Finally, I had to let him know the truth, that for nearly three years now, Ruby was living with me.

My brother was actually able to get out of prison early because he found out that Ruby was not with her mother and that I was here trying to take care of two children. He must have had a fit in prison. After finding out for certain that she was with me, they let him out early to care for her. So, Janine took Ruby back to show my brother that they could once again be a big happy family. At this time, however, Janine and Ruby were actually living with Janine's family. There were six of them in all, including her youngest brother, Ruby's cousin, who was a little older than Ruby. As it turned out, Ruby told me that her cousin was sexually abusing her. Usually Ruby was left alone in a room, and he would go to "play with her." But it was not just innocent playing. He would be doing other things and when Janine found out, she had a big fight with her mother over why she wasn't watching him. Her cousin apologized to Ruby but when my brother found out he made sure to get them out of that house.

Somehow when he came out of prison he was immediately able to get a job with some temp agency. He knew the people at the agency so they found him something quickly, and he used the money to get a room for Janine and Ruby. For the moment Janine was happy, thinking that now she had finally gotten what she wanted, my brother. However, it was not to be, as my brother did not want to stay with them. Instead he stayed at my house. He would help them out financially, and with Janine still collecting welfare, they could get along fine. He didn't want to be there and risk fighting with her or having any kind of trouble that might land him back in jail.

By this time, Ruby was supposed to be in third grade, but once again was not going to school. Janine wasn't doing much of anything as a parent so my brother tried to get Janine to sign custody over to me. She refused and I explained to him that he could not force her. The best thing he could do was to simply keep on working and visit them every day. So he did just that, and checked up on Ruby every day. Pretty soon Janine and Ruby left the room he had set up for them and moved back in with her family, which upset him even more, but he had to keep his cool.

Moving forward a few years, social services eventually helped Janine get her own place in the Bronx where she and Ruby moved in. Ruby became a very troubled teenager. She did not attend school very often and was out with her friends most of the time. When she did go to school she would get into fights and cut classes. The principal told my brother that she was cursing everybody out. She also joined a gang and started having sex at around the age of thirteen. Ruby was angry and out of control and her mother made no attempt to do anything about it.

At thirteen, Ruby moved out. Janine didn't tell my brother at first. Once again, he would ask her where Ruby was and why she never got on the phone but Janine kept on making things up. Finally, I went over and asked, "Where is Ruby?"

She told me she kept trying to talk to my brother and explain but he was always yelling and screaming at her. Even though I knew it wouldn't help the situation, I couldn't blame him for being angry with Janine. She never took care of Ruby from the time she was born. Janine finally told me that Ruby was living with a twenty-one year old boy and gave me an address that Ruby had given her. Apparently, the boy's father had an apartment and was letting his son stay there. But when my brother went to find her, of course the address didn't check out. I honestly don't think Janine had any clue where Ruby and this boy were living.

At some point Ruby got a Facebook account, and she connected with my daughter. It was the only way we knew she was okay. My brother finally contacted her and she told him that she was not trying to be disrespectful. She explained that Janine allowed her to stay with the boy, knowing he was twenty-one, so she could run the streets with various men.

Finally, after a long search, my brother found Ruby, packed up her stuff and made her move with him to Woodside in Queens where he had just gotten a place with his new girlfriend. At this point Ruby was nearly sixteen and he had no idea what he was in for. He made her go to school and thought everything would be better. But it didn't take long for Ruby to start being disrespectful to the principal and the teachers. Then, one night when my brother was asleep, thinking his daughter was at home and in her bed, he heard noise in the hallway, so he got up to see what was going on. Ruby was bent over with some boy.

My brother tried to take control but Ruby wouldn't have any part of it. She would tell him, "You ain't been here all these years and now you suddenly want to play daddy?"

Then she started running away practically every night and he'd have to look for her on the streets of Woodside, a neighborhood he was unfamiliar with. He decided that before she got herself raped or killed, he would send her back to her mother. She stayed with her mom for a week then went back to the boy who was now twenty-four. As it turned out, he was actually only a few blocks away from her mother's house. The last I heard of Ruby, she got tossed out by the boy and returned to her Janine's home.

Ruby was neglected from day one. I did what I could because it pained me to see her in such bad shape. The only reason Janine didn't let me sign the papers to be her legal guardian was in hopes that she could have this magical family life with my brother and their daughter. When that didn't work out, Ruby was tossed aside.

Another story I came across was about a child whose mother had children to try and keep a very abusive man she should have let go a long time ago, now Katie lived in Boston along with her mother Liz and father Charles, in the beginning everything was ok, Katie's mother had 5 more kids with the same man but this man had lots of women on the side and sold drugs on the street. After about 5 years of living in Boston with Liz, Katie's father wanted to take his drug selling to the next level so he moved to Philadelphia with hopes of making more money because the family was getting bigger. He promised Katie's mom that he would return in a year for her and the kids, but a year had come and gone and Katie's father had not returned. Katie's mother decided to drop all her kids at their grandfathers house an go and search for the father in Philly, she had heard him mention several streets he sold on, while eavesdropping on a few of his conversation with his boss. When Katie's mother found Charles she found out he had another child with another women and he had moved in with his new family. With anger and retaliation on her mind Katie's mother got and apartment in the same building as the other women and showed up at the women's door with pictures of her children she had with Charles. The women told Liz that she didn't know anything about Charles having another family elsewhere and asked Liz to leave her apartment because Liz had begun to get really loud and began to push and shove the women. Later, that day Liz heard loud bangs on her new apt door and when she opened it. It was Charles, he wanted to know how did she find him and how long had she been staying there without his knowledge, she told him don't worry about that, start talking about this new family. Before Charles could speak Liz smack Charles and ask him how could he do this to them, Charles was shocked by the quick left hand and smacked and kicked Liz in the stomach and told her go home with his kids. This wasn't the first time Liz and Charles had fought, one time he beat Liz so bad her family was not sure it was her when they showed up to the hospital. So Liz knew Charles would hit her back but she felt like this is a way he showed he cared.

The next morning Liz left the apt and headed back to Boston, Charles thought she had given up the apt and decided to move on with her life being that she found out about his new family, about 3 days later Liz returned with all her kids, she made sure she stopped at Charles new family's home and showed the women all of Charles kids from Boston, the women slammed the door in Liz face and yelled get away from my door, about 30 minutes later Charles banged on the door and asked Liz what the hell is she doing and why did she just up and move the kids there, what about school? Where are all their clothes? What happened to the apt in Boston? Liz just looked at Charles and said where ever you go I go, I will not live without you. Charles grabbed Liz by the collar and began choking her while demanding her to go back home, Liz oldest son and daughter tried to fight their father because there mother was screaming get off of me, the oldest son started punching

Charles and the oldest daughter began to pull Charles hair and scratch Charles in the face as hard and deep as she could to make Charles stop choking their mother, Charles turned around an hit both kids as hard as he could knocking both of them completely out. Liz began screaming my kids you killed my kids, hearing the sounds of their mothers screams the kids began to wake up. Charles fled the apt.

Liz had blamed the oldest kids for their fathers attack on her and told them that everything that has happened as far as their father leaving and getting a new family was their fault, she also began yelling "if you f-cking kids weren't so bad, he would have stayed with us", she grabbed lipstick out her purse and began to write on the walls that she hated kids, and without Charles, her life meant nothing.

It's Not a New Phenomenon

Many women were, and still are raised to find a man and have a family. The more ingrained it is by their parents (usually by their moms), the more desperate they may become for love and a relationship – and this type of "trapping a man" behavior is typically an act of desperation. In fact, another reason why women try to trap a man into staying with them, or marrying them, is because they desperately want to get out of their family's home. Sadly, even girls in middle school have resorted to such tricks to escape living at home.

In reality, women have done this for years. I read a story written by a fifty year old woman who got pregnant to trap a man when she was just fourteen. The story didn't say what kind of mom she turned out to be once the baby was born. The couple, however, did not stay together.

In some cases a child does help maintain the relationship. Typically it's not the healthiest way to keep a relationship going, but on occasion the couple does learn to love each other. This is the exception. In most circumstances such a plan does not work. Yet, women continue to try such tactics. Often, women who are responsible for using birth control conveniently, "forget" to use it, telling their man they don't need to wear a condom since they have everything under control. Then, when they do get pregnant, they blame it on faulty birth control. In other cases women have even tampered with condoms in an attempt to get pregnant.

Some women who have tried such tricks realize that their partner was one step out the door while they were still pregnant, and then made adoption plans, knowing that they were not ready to raise a child alone. Others shift their love from their man to their baby and make a conscious effort to raise their child with or without a man. While it's not easy being a single parent, these women take on the challenge and basically say, "The hell with him, I have a baby now." In these cases, the children are fortunate to grow up with a loving parent.

Of course we cannot let the men completely off the hook here – women aren't the only ones who manipulate the situation to have a kid. A phone survey by the National Domestic Violence Hotline revealed that 25 percent of women have claimed that a partner had pressured them to become pregnant. Some were just pushy, while others found excuses not to wear condoms and some, like the women mentioned above, even punctured the condoms. Another survey showed that 75 percent of women who claimed to be in an abusive relationship, reported that the men tried to use some type of coercion to get them pregnant.

Options besides Neglecting the Child

Whether the woman is at fault for using a child to trap a man or the man is at fault for talking a woman into getting pregnant, if the result is a child, someone has to act responsibly. Once you have a child, you cannot simply say, "Well my plan didn't work out." Then go ahead and neglect your child. That is how we get more deadbeat parents. Calling social services can help, if they evaluate the situation and see that the mom is not prepared to be a parent. In the case of Ruby, social services should have found out where Ruby was and whether or not she was being cared for. They should have seen that at age three or four she was seriously behind in her development. They were giving money to Janine, so they should have found out about her daughter.

Visiting Janine's home and looking around, they would have seen, before I did, that Ruby could not walk or talk and was on formula and in diapers until she was almost four years old. I wish I had been persistent and tried to see her more often between the ages of two and four, but I was busy raising my own daughter.

Social services, however, needs to stay on top of these situations and act earlier. One of the problems is that women like Janine are scared that if they find the child, the mother will be punished. While the mother should be punished, if they can get her to sign over custody by promising her that she won't get into trouble, then they should do just that. The best interest of the child should come first. The other problem that arises is that it is too easy to manipulate the system to get money or hold onto a child for the wrong reasons.

No, I do not like to see families broken up by social services. But deadbeat, neglectful moms need to be stopped early on while the children are young enough to find a better life elsewhere.

CHAPTER 7

Child Exploitation

Former model and talk show host, Tyra Banks, aired episodes of her television program on which she had parents (usually mothers) who wanted more than anything to have their children, even toddlers, succeed in show business. Some had only good intentions, while others were hoping to vicariously capture the stardom that they were never able to attain. Still others were looking for a meal ticket in the form of their child.

On one show, in fact, Banks actually asked parents if they would allow plastic surgery to be performed on their child to enhance their appearance – some replied that they would, even on a child as young as three! And then there are the beauty pageants that put little girls, even babies against one another for the sake of the mom's egos and, usually, cash.

A recent study from the Journal of the American Academy of Child and Adolescent Psychiatry discussed the exploits within the glitzy $5 billion child reality pageant industry. The author, Martina M. Cartwright, Ph.D., a registered dietician and adjunct professor in the University of Arizona's department of nutritional sciences, wrote that "high-glitz child pageants - largely popularized by the TLC hit reality show Toddlers and Tiaras and its spin-off, Here Comes Honey Boo Boo - often have little to do with the children and much more to do with satisfying the needs of their parents." She goes on to suggest that such pageants can be harmful to children's health and self-esteem.

Having attended two tapings of "Toddlers and Tiaras," Cartwright wrote that some pageant parents exhibit what she calls "princess by proxy," a unique form of "achievement by proxy distortion" in which adults are driven primarily by the social or financial gains earned by their child's accomplishments, regardless of any risks involved for the child. She also points to the high costs involved in the heavy makeup, ornate costumes, artificial teeth, fake tans and so on that these little girls are subjected to.

No matter what you call it, this is a form of child exploitation. However, as misguided as this type of exploitation may sound, it pales in comparison to sexual exploitation of children. I read a study that estimated that over 300,000 children in the United States, Canada and Mexico run the risk of becoming victims of sexual exploitation every year. What this particular study did not mention is the surprisingly high number of children who are exploited by their own mothers. Yes, another type of deadbeat mom is the one that exploits her own child to make money, receive "gifts" or support the family.

Many people assume that child prostitution is the result of runaways desperately trying to support a drug habit. The assumption is that these kids have made a conscious choice to follow this path, perhaps as a last ditch effort to make some money and stay as far away from their families as long as possible. Statistics, however, indicate that more than half of teenage prostitutes were coerced into the lifestyle, many by their own parents.

Marietta's Story

I met Marietta in the local playground. My daughter was about five, and she loved going on the swings and down the slide. Marietta was several years older, a teenager, with dark brown hair, light brown eyes and an olive complexion. She was very beautiful despite being a bit of a tomboy. On days when other teenagers were not around, she would come to the playground and sit on one of the benches. At first we chatted about the neighborhood, and then little by little, about her life. She was mild mannered and sweet. She talked about being a young gay Latino woman in a world that was difficult for women,

Latinos and gays. She added that she also liked boys, and that it was easier dating them.

She seemed very mature in her manner and very well spoken for a fifteen year old. I sensed from our conversations that she, like myself, had been through some very difficult times. She talked often about how much she hated her mother and as we got to know each other better she told me that she saw the way I took care of my daughter and played with her, and that she wished I was her mother.

The more often we saw each other, the more she opened up and told me about her home life. She seemed to trust me and one day the floodgates opened. Her mom, Josephine, whom I later realized that I had seen around the neighborhood, was always drunk. She had Marietta when she was fifteen and was now a single mom living in nearby Spanish Harlem. Every dollar she received, often from handouts, would go to buying alcohol. Marietta would beg her mother for money to buy new clothes, but Josephine rarely ever had money to feed her, let alone buy clothes. Marietta would go to school in old clothes and worn down shoes.

For Josephine to maintain her alcohol habit, she would "entertain" different men at her house. Marietta would stay quietly in her room, while strange men would come and go. One man in particular, Jose, who had known Josephine for at least four years, was a frequent visitor and stayed over at their house very often.

Marietta explained that Jose would always ask her to come and sit on his lap and her mother would tell her not to be frightened and that it was okay. So, she'd sit on his lap. In time, this escalated from sitting on his lap to him asking her to rub his back, his feet, and give him a kiss. Each time he asked for something new her mother would okay it. The more Jose stayed at the house the more groceries Marietta would see come into their home. Josephine even bought Marietta a dress with matching shoes, so Marietta continued to do as her mother told her and honor Jose's requested.

When Marietta turned fifteen, Jose asked her to go out dancing with him. She declined, but her mother reminded her of where all of the food and new clothes were coming from. So Marietta, at fifteen, started going out dancing with a man in his forties who in turn started giving her money. He told her not to tell her mother. She did not, and confessed that she was actually enjoying the attention. She had never met her father and this was the first male to show her any real attention, in fact it was the first time anyone had been nice to her.

There were several fashionable dance clubs in upper Manhattan and they would go on Saturday nights. During the week, Marietta was in high school and often sitting in the park in the afternoons, sometimes reading her schoolbooks. On occasion she would play with my daughter and I could see her laughing and having fun. It was nice to see Marietta smile, since she so often looked sad at her predicament, with a mom who had time for men and alcohol but no time for her. Clothes and food notwithstanding, Marietta knew she needed to be nice to Jose primarily to get what her mom needed for her own personal gains.

Then it turned ugly...

I remember that there was a two-week stretch during which I did not see Marietta, who was pretty much a regular at the playground. While my daughter and I played, or she played with her friends, I glanced around but Marietta wasn't there. About a week later I saw her again. Apparently the attention she was receiving from Jose had turned ugly when Marietta's mom insisted that, on the way to dinner one night, they join him at a somewhat sleazy Manhattan hotel.

Marietta did not want to go and made it clear she would wait for them outside.

The situation escalated and when Marietta started to cry, Jose grabbed her, and along with her mother, they literally dragged her into the hotel room. She explained that she tried to fight them off, but wasn't strong enough. Before she knew it they undressed her, and Jose raped her while her own mother watched!

Her mother sold Marietta for an unknown sum of money. The following day, she left home and was staying at a friend's house. That would be temporary because she was scared that her mother or Jose would find her and abuse her again. It was the last time I saw Marietta for a number of years.

Not long ago, I saw a pregnant woman in the neighborhood who looked very familiar. It was Marietta. She was now in her mid-twenties. She had tried to reconcile with her mother and move back home, but her mother wanted nothing to do with her and threw her out. She was alone, scared and hungry. I didn't want to pry into her life but asked if she wanted to stay at my house until she found someplace more permanent. She declined the offer and told me she'd be okay at the local shelter for a while. I gave her some money for food. She smiled and hugged me. She whispered that she had been stealing money from her mother whenever she had the chance. She never called the authorities on her mom, but this was her way of getting back at her, although it would never make up for what her mother did to her. I didn't ask her about the pregnancy but offered to be there if she needed someone to help her with the baby. I haven't seen or heard from Marietta since.

I wish Marietta had called the authorities on her mom but I could understand her fear. It's hard to build a case against someone, especially a relative, unless other people step up to support your story. The fear of retaliation is great and there is still some weird bond with a parent that stops you from turning them in. No matter how many times I wanted to turn my mother in to the authorities, I was always scared to do so; I always had a soft spot for her and always thought someday she would change. Kids in these situations need guidance. They need someone they can trust to talk to, whether it's a social worker, the local priest or a friend. They need someone who they can rely on to go with them to the authorities if necessary. Unfortunately, left to their own devices, kids will not always know what the good and bad choices are, when they look for someone to confide in. Too many people are not trustworthy and will take advantage of children - very sad, but true.

While I felt bad for Marietta, it also made me feel that I wasn't alone. In fact, I sort of felt like I was part of a group, a group of women whose own mothers turned the other way and refused to recognize the hideous sexual abuse of their daughters. Or, in Marietta's case, they actually took part in it.

I always thought I was the only person that had gone through this type of situation with my mom and my stepmom, both of whom knew my stepfather was raping me, but never helped me at all. I never talked to other people about it, not even a therapist. I didn't know whom I could turn to and trust. I hope Marietta found someone who could be of help to her and found a way to release some of the anger and pain she felt toward her mother. I hope she remembered how I acted with my daughter and followed that example when her baby was born.

Cindy's Story

Sadly, stories like Marietta's are not as unique as one might think. Dr. Casey recounts a similar story from a woman he saw in his practice. It was Cindy's second session when she mentioned that whenever she saw a piano she would get nauseated. Cindy explained that her mom insisted that she learn how to play piano as a child. So, starting at the age of eight, she took lessons and by twelve she had become quite good.

"My mom forced me to practice hours and hours to the point of exhaustion and if I stopped for any reason she would always hit the back of my hands with her wire hairbrush. To this day I remember vividly the look of the back of my hands from being hit… And I remember the excruciating pain," explained Cindy.

Her parents had divorced when she was two years old and she never saw her father again. She moved with her mom from county to county along with an ongoing string of men that her mom met, usually at local bars.

Cindy's nightmare began one evening when her mom came into her room, intoxicated, dragged her to the piano and demanded her to play. Frightened and confused, she did not argue and started playing the piano. A few minutes later she realized that her mom and some man were having sex right behind where she was playing.

"I didn't understand what was happening," said Cindy, adding that it felt like a bad dream.

Pretty soon this type of activity became a routine. Most Friday nights, Cindy's mom came home drunk from a bar and had her daughter play piano while she had sex. Frightened and horrified, Cindy complied. She kept her head down and serenaded her mom and the male visitor.

It proceeded to get worse for Cindy the night after her thirteenth birthday. "My mom came home with a biker guy. And as expected, she told me in her usual slurred speech, to play the piano. When I was halfway through, she told me to take my clothes off. I was frozen stiff, and pretended I didn't hear her. Shortly after, she screamed at me.

'"Don't make me come over there and rip them off your body!"' My mother shouted.

"I saw the biker guy lying there naked and smirking. I closed my eyes and got undressed. Then I played a couple of songs," explained Cindy.

From there the horrors continued. She was asked to give the boyfriend a back rub. Before long, he was touching her as she prayed the experience would end. Fortunately for Cindy it did shortly thereafter. But the pattern had begun and her mother started pushing her to the boyfriends in order to keep them around. Gradually this became a regular occurrence in the house with her mother bringing new guys home and forcing her to strip, play piano, dance and have sex while her mom would sit there drinking alcohol. Cindy was having recurring nightmares by the time she was fourteen years old. She also started gaining a lot of weight in hopes that she would be less appealing to the boyfriends. “One of the worst beatings I ever got from my mom was when I refused to strip for one of her boyfriends,” says Cindy.

Afterwards she was consumed with the idea of running away. While Cindy didn’t actually run away, she was able to stay at her friends’ houses. She let her mother know that she talked with her new friends about all kinds of things so that they were aware of the situation. Occasionally, when her friends were not around, she stayed in local shelters.

Years later, after working very hard in school, Cindy opened three businesses that were all extremely successful. She found pleasure in working very hard and also helping others. Over 95 % of the employees were female and came from various shelters.

Meanwhile, for many years she avoided any kind of relationship with a man and turned down all dating requests. The idea of having sex with men was a scary notion. Then, at the age of 35, she fell in love with a man but due to her fears, they decided to go to therapy. After about a year, she got married, but she had no interest in having a child.

A Serious Dilemma

Child exploitation and trafficking is a worldwide problem. Some of the trafficking can be directly linked to parents. Often they are deadbeat moms, who use their children as a means of getting what they should be attaining for themselves. This could be money or just attention from men.

Stories like Marietta's or Cindy's or that of another woman who essentially traded her teenage daughter to her landlord in exchange for a month's rent, shock and outrage most of society. And yet, such activity takes place worldwide. In fact, in 2005, in France, the largest and most horrific trial of its kind saw 66 people appear in a courtroom, accused of prostituting and sexually abusing 45 children under the age of twelve. The defendants included parents and grandparents accused of "selling" their children or grandchildren for small amounts of money, food, cigarettes, and, in one case, a new tire.

While some think this is the kind of thing that could never happen in America, it does happen, and too often involves the mother. In most cases these deadbeat mothers are "sociopaths with narcissistic tendencies," explains Dr. Casey. He adds that, "They have no interest in having a baby since the baby represents a burden and requires giving. Many of the pregnancies are a mistake and become a matter of inconvenience with nine months of hatred, resentfulness and inability to bond. They see their child as their property, an object to increase their grandiose thinking. As a result, they use their own children to better themselves by earning money or helping them keep a man. After all, why should their children have a good life when they have been such a burden? Interestingly, the outward expression of these women tends to be fun and playful, which draws men to them. Yet they are really hostile, distant and have contempt for others including, and especially, their children." Such hostility and resentment leads to some astonishing behavior as exemplified by Marietta and Cindy's deadbeat moms who tried to provide for themselves by prostituting their own daughters.

Another Type of Exploitation

A personal situation made me aware of another rather unusual way of exploiting one's own children: **fighting**.

One Sunday morning, my daughter went to the Laundromat to do our laundry. The attendant on duty at the time was a short African American woman, maybe in her late 40s who walked around eyeballing the young women. When these female customers would question why she was checking them out, she would start cursing them and calling them all sorts of names. Then, when the situation would appear to escalate to the verge of a fight, she would call her daughters to get into a street fight with the women from the Laundromat. She was either making money by betting on the fight, having her daughters steal money from the victim or she simply liked watching women fight, so she used her daughters who were 17 and 21 as her fighters.

When my daughter was being called all sorts of names by this evil little woman, she texted me and asked me to come downstairs. When I showed up at the Laundromat, the woman changed her tune and backed off. Her daughters who were hanging around outside waiting to fight my daughter also backed off when they saw that she wasn't alone. Once I was outside with my daughter, I talked with them. Then the 21 year old told me she'd already been to jail three times for assault because of her mom. The other one said she'd been arrested four times thanks to her mom. They both added that they were sick of it but that their mother forced them to do it because she kept telling them, "I'm your mother and not only are you supposed to listen to me, and you are supposed to protect me right or wrong." I told them that they were old enough to make their own choices and if they didn't want to go back to jail, perhaps it was time to say “no” to mom. I have no idea if they listened. In an effort to keep my daughter out of harm’s way, we simply started using a different Laundromat.

International Exploitation

Deadbeat mothers are also in different parts of the world, as I spoke about earlier in my book, some of these countries are places we dream about visiting like: China, Jamaica, Bahamas, Argentina, and Ghana. The number one exploitation that goes on in these parts is

Sex trafficking:

Liu (**China**) has a daughter name Chi, Chi is only 10 years old and she has to make money for her family every day. 8am every morning Liu sends her daughter out to sell fish, Chi is told if she cannot make a certain amount of money selling fish to the visitors she will have to sleep with strange men; Chi is afraid but does it because her mother tells her that this a something she must do to help feed her smaller brothers and sisters. I call this a disgrace how dear her mother sells her child’s body for pennies but this is one of the realities that go on around the world.

Shelly (**Nassau**), now shelly is in the 8th grade and has a crush on a class mate name Duran he is tall, dark and beautiful and Shelly rushes to school each day to see him,

Duran and Shelly begins to date behind her mother's back, Shelly's mother finds out through the small community about their relationship, Shelly's mother demands Shelly to stop dating Duran and began dating an older man that her mother claims will help feed the family and pay the bills and occasionally buy her mother dresses and costume jewelry for party nights, Shelly tells her mother" the man you want me to date is your age", but her mother reminds Shelly that the Leader of the country has change the legal age to 16 years old for girls; so do as I say. Shelly being defiant says to her mother "You know the only reason why the Leader changed the legal age to 16 is because one of his friends got a 16 year old girl pregnant, but before that happened the legal age was 18 years old". Shelly's mom smacked Shelly in the face and told her if she didn't date this child predator that she would have to leave the house; with nowhere to go and no one to turn to Shelly dates this man. Stories like this breaks my heart, now I can honestly say my mother has never asked me in any way shape of form to sleep with men to support her drug addiction, I thank god for that, but this has got to stop.

Zaira (**Argentina)** Zaira is a 4 years old child and is being left in the home alone every day by her mother so her mother can work, her mother works long hours and by the time she reaches home, Zaira is passed out because she has not eaten or drank any water in hours. This is a situation that has been going on for the last 2 years. Zaira wants to cry when she finally wakes up and sees her mother but dares to because she know what will happen to her, so Zaira kindly just walks to her mom with a sad face an gives a welcome home hug. Now, the reason Zaira does not cry is because in Argentina I have learned that when a child is born he/she is dipped in scalding hot water when they cry, and dipped in the river as they get older; this is done to make the children strong and obedient. Even though, this seems like some type of ritual, this is abuse at its finest, ritual or not I could not ever think of putting a child in scalding hot water, let's pray for these children and hope with time this will stop.

What to do?

When I look at my daughter, who's all grown up now, and I think of how hard I worked to protect her from anyone who would want to harm her, it makes me sick to think of the deadbeat moms who can go so far as exploit their own children. Aren't parents supposed to protect their children? Even in the animal kingdom, mothers guard their young from predators.

Unfortunately, unless the exploited child confides in someone, nobody will help. And too often they are afraid of being beaten or harmed more seriously if their mothers or even their mothers' boyfriends find out that they have spoken up. I wanted Marietta to report her mom. I even offered to go with her but she said "No." She feared that not only would she not get any help but that her mom or Jose would come after her and beat her, or worse.

Unlike abuse that one witnesses and reports to the authorities, this type of abuse goes on behind closed doors and is humiliating and paralyzing. Often the scars are emotional with no visible signs. You want to speak up, but you can't. You want to tell someone but you don't know whom you can trust. Believe me, I know. Yet I encourage victims to seek out someone they can trust or look for local services in their communities where abused teenagers can turn.

Outsiders who are aware of such situations typically do not come forward for fear that they are getting involved where they do not belong, in someone else's family matters. They may also be reluctant to speak up in a small community where there could be repercussions.

I wish I had helped Marietta, but I could only offer my support. When talking with a teenager, it's harder to do something unless they want you to. If however, you know that a young child is being exploited or molested, you should talk to the authorities and let them know what evidence you have to suspect something is wrong. You can speak up anonymously about exploitation, abuse or anything you know that is jeopardizing the wellbeing of a child.

Take some time to call, or walk into, social services or the local police station and ask to talk with someone about what you have seen or heard. Depending on whom you speak to you may get someone sympathetic to the plight of these children. Or, you may hear the response, "Kids tend to exaggerate, "or" We can't act unless you have more evidence."

This usually means the person to whom you are speaking doesn't really want to be involved. Sadly, even people who should be aware of such exploitation don't totally believe what really goes on out there. If you get such a response, go and talk to someone else. See if you can find someone willing to listen. A few hours of your time could save a child.

CHAPTER 8
What to do About Deadbeat Moms

There comes a time in life, when you need to step up and take action. When Tanya's two young children continually asked for food, I helped out. But when I confronted Tanya about her neglect and also about the brother's inappropriate touching of his younger sister, Tanya took it out on the little girl. I felt terrible. I knew she was a neglectful mom, and now realized that she was also abusive, yet I didn't know what I could do about it.

The problem is that when you become aware of an inappropriate situation it becomes hard to figure out what your next move should be. How do you go about reporting the situation and to whom do you report it?

If you speak up, the mother may take it out on the child, as if he or she is to blame (as in the case of Tanya). If you don't speak up, you know the child's situation will not improve and may only get worse. I've learned a lot since that time and I am now more comfortable speaking up if I think something is wrong. However, it's not always easy to do. Clearly there are a lot of factors involved in exposing deadbeat moms for who they really are. And as we've illustrated in the previous chapters, there are a few different types of deadbeat moms to contend with. The overriding theme that continues to prevail is simply that deadbeat moms exist in larger numbers than the media wants to broadcast. Even several literary agents and publishers responded to this book by saying, “It is just another book about abuse.”

This indicates that they’ve been there and done that already. While there are books by leading scholars and "so called" experts in the field, there are still tons of reports about mothers abandoning their children or worse. The problem hasn’t gone away. In fact, if anything, deadbeat moms who are not taking financial responsibility have increased in recent years, while cases of neglect and abuse overload the child welfare bureaus. According to some, the experts have spoken, the books have been written, and the problem no longer matters. Tell that to the child who is malnourished, beaten or abandoned. Ignoring an issue or deciding that it’s no longer the hot trendy issue of the day, doesn’t make it go away.

That’s why I wrote this book, posted my **website (www.deadbeatmomstories.com)** and want to help abused, neglected children, because the problem **HAS NOT** been resolved and should no longer be swept under the rug. I too consider myself an expert in the field. While I don't have the diploma, I have the scars. Right now there are campaigns all over the media about breast cancer awareness, which is terrific. However, the HIV virus, which was all over the media at one time, is also still killing people but receives far less attention – it's not the issue of the day.

Likewise, we hear very little about destructive deadbeat moms. Do we need to wait until there is some nationally covered horror story about a deadbeat mom, like the Casey Anthony story, for people to remember that child neglect and abuse is still around us? It's sad that attention to real issues that affect millions of people comes and goes like fashion trends, even when the problems still exist.

Tell a poor neglected, abused, deprived child that he or she will have to wait until abuse and neglect become trendy topics once again for news producers and editors to act. I wrote this book and had it published to put the topic out there for those who understand that this remains a very real problem.

Too many moms get a free pass, despite their actions, while dads pay or end up in jail. Fathers are accused of abuse while moms are overlooked and allowed to raise their children as they wish. Sure there are deadbeat and abusive men out there.

Newsflash: There are also deadbeat and abusive mothers, plenty of them, I know first-hand.

What Can You Do About It?

Let's start off talking about the abusive, neglectful deadbeat moms. First, you need to have a reason to suspect someone of being a deadbeat mom. A child like Ruby made it pretty clear to me that neglect was taking place. It is not always that obvious. Nor is it easy to talk to the mother.

I already knew Ruby's mom because she was my brother's girlfriend. In the case of Tanya, it was clear she wanted nothing to do with me. I was glad to hear that her daughter's father recognized her neglectful partying ways and took his daughter away from her.

There are obvious signs that a child might be being abused, such as bruises, welts, swellings, sprains, burns, abrasions or even torn or bloodied clothing. These may also be signs that a child is fighting or being bullied at school. If that is the case, these signs should fade once a responsible parent is aware of the situation. Continued signs of abuse are more likely coming from the home environment. If a child has trouble walking or sitting this could also be a sign of sexual abuse.

The problem for you, as someone who is concerned for the child, is that you do not want to jump to any conclusions nor do you want to call social services if you do not know the facts.

Signs of a parent's neglect may be easier to notice than signs of abuse. Kids may appear to be unsupervised, malnourished, inappropriately dressed for the cold weather, or wearing clothing that does not fit them. They may have poor hygiene or be clingy to people who are not their parents.

In some cases of neglect or abuse, they may not want to go home after school or after playing. I've seen children who wanted desperately to stay in the playground rather than go home with their moms to what was likely a beating for some reason—one that might have had nothing to do with the child.

Reporting these situations is where it becomes very difficult. I remember reading a blog by a man who saw a woman hitting her two young children on a public bus. After a while he couldn't take it anymore and he yelled at her, telling her if she didn't stop he would call the police.

There were a number of other people on the bus and they were simply watching her or pretending not to notice as she backhanded and punched her kids. At the next stop, she grabbed her kids and got off the bus spitting at the man before leaving and yelling a few choice words.

Someone else commented to him that she was "f--ked up." The next day he called the police, not to report her, since he had no idea who she was, but simply to ask what could be done in such a situation. The police were unsure, telling him that it's a touchy, murky, delicate situation, all of which essentially meant that they really didn't know what someone could or should do. And this is the problem... What do you do?

If you are convinced that a child is being harmed or neglected you can call social services and file an anonymous report. However, this may not help the situation since social services may take a long time to investigate and in the end not have enough evidence to do anything about it. There are numerous stories of social services going to a home and not finding anything, because they speak only to the mother who is not going to admit that anything is wrong.

Unless you witness the problem firsthand on a regular basis or it is obvious, such as the case with Ruby, the mother can always claim that the child got into a fight at school or that someone else is the culprit if the child appears injured in some manner. In many cases the social service workers do not even talk to the child. Most deadbeat moms know how to put on a show to make everything appear okay when they need to.

My foster mom was a witch, but when she had to make everything appear fine, she could do so. She kept up the act just long enough to make sure she would get her money for keeping us in her little hell camp. And that's just what happens far too often. The neglectful or abusive mom plays the teary eyed victim who is stressed, but loves her children and only wants what's best for them. Then as soon as the social workers are out the door, she goes back to being the deadbeat abusive, neglectful mom that she really is.
Nonetheless, if you have good reason to believe something is wrong, you can try reporting the mother—see the appendix for phone numbers and suggestions of places to call. BUT, if she knows you've called the authorities on her, be careful. This is why people do not want to get involved. They fear for their own safety and that of the children—you do not want to make things worse, so make sure to remain anonymous.

Another option is to try to befriend the person if they are a neighbor or someone you have met before. This is more time consuming, but if you can get to know the deadbeat mom and gain her confidence, you might be able to find out what is going on and offer to help her out if possible.

Perhaps when she's neglecting her children, you can provide some babysitting or some meals as I did. If you are worried about physical abuse, you can talk about ways in which you handle such situations without bringing up what you suspect she is doing.

Be a helpful friend and maybe you can get her to let you help her out. Do not accuse someone, do not preach and do not push your way into a situation if someone does not want to talk or befriend you. The point is, if you can become a confidant, then perhaps you can provide a positive influence or lead her to professional help. These are possibilities, but none of them are easy. Very often deadbeat moms are very well set in their ways and not amenable to change.

You may seek some outside help. If you confide in a member of the church, such as your pastor or talk with a social worker, or even someone in the school whom you know you can trust, perhaps they can provide you with some ideas of how to help this child. Someone in the school can also be on the lookout. She can see if there is anything unusual about the child's appearance or behavior. In some cases, teachers have been able to intervene in a family situation. In many cases, however, they may provide advice, but otherwise, do not want to get involved.

Of course it would be great if you could get the deadbeat mom to talk to someone who could be of help, but it's unlikely that they will listen unless they are ready to acknowledge that they are doing something wrong. People do not accept help until they recognize that there is a problem. This explains why so many people refuse to go to rehab when they have a substance abuse problem.

It's Not Easy

It's easy to do nothing, which is why so many children are abused. People simply do not want to get involved - BUT if a child's wellbeing is at stake and you know how he or she is being treated, you owe it to that child to try to do something if you can. They say it takes a village to raise a child and in this case, that village is made up of the people who recognize when a child is in trouble.

In some cases spreading the word amongst others in your community, or in the neighborhood, people who see the child on a regular basis, may generate some overall concern. There is safety in numbers and you may not be approaching the situation alone. Not that you are going to have an intervention, but if a few people approach a deadbeat mom in a helpful manner, it might be easier to get the point across.

It was the community that told my dad that my brother and I were living with our mom in a burnt out abandoned building. There are many good people who want to help if they know something is wrong, especially when it involves children.

Why People Don't Get Involved

Along with being concerned for their own safety, there are other reasons why people don't get involved. There is the very real connection between a mother and her child that is difficult to break. Most people do not want to be responsible for breaking up a family. Even though in some cases it is in the best interest of the child to do so, there is the feeling that the deadbeat mom will come to her senses.

As you can see from my story, I gave my mom chance after chance after chance to change and finally take responsibility as a parent or even as a grandparent. She failed me time and time again though I kept hoping she would change. Many of us try very hard to find the positive side and never want to stop hoping that things will get better. Unfortunately, for many children, they do not get better, the situation never changes, and they suffer through the only childhood they have. Another reason why people do not get involved is because there is a sense that other people have different ways of raising their children and disciplining them. However, it's not all that difficult to differentiate between a parent spanking a child on the rear end or slapping his or her hand and someone who is out of control whaling away on a child.

If you know the parent and child, and see them on a regular basis, you can tell if the child looks frightened of the parent most of the time. If the child is walking on eggshells, always scared of setting off the parent, you know something is wrong. Interestingly, we are very quick to notice abusive behavior in fathers, but not in mothers. When we see violent, demeaning or humiliating behavior coming from fathers directed at their children, we are outraged, but when it is the mother, society just seems to let it slide. A young child can be just as badly hurt, physically and emotionally, from a mother as a father.

It's also easy to recognize when a parent is taking out anger over something the child was not responsible for and hitting them. Discipline should be a way of teaching a child not to do something or not to behave in a certain manner. That's totally different from someone taking out anger and frustration on a child.

Parents often use control or fear to give them leverage and to keep children in line. Fear of losing privileges or even getting a spanking may be a means of discipline for some parents. Fear of a serious beating, however, is crossing the line. If my daughter is fearful that I won't let her go somewhere with her friends, she may be upset, but it's still based on my concern for her and the fact that I love her. She is not fearful that I am going to do her serious physical injury. There is a huge difference here. You can tell when parents repeatedly threaten beatings, which may indicate a problem.

Another reason why so many people steer clear of problems such as child abuse and neglect is that they simply don't have the time to get involved. Before reporting someone to child welfare or speaking to the individual, you need to make sure you are on the right track. You'll need to take some time to gather some facts to determine if there is a pattern of abuse or neglect. It's up to you to determine whether or not you can invest some time to help a child out. Remember, children need advocates on their behalf. I wish I had had one when I was growing up.

One very common reason why people may not get involved is because it's happening in their own family.

"No, this type of behavior doesn't happen in our family." This is a poor but common excuse for why people sit on the sidelines. Perhaps they don't want to acknowledge that someone is out of control or they may have their own motive for not getting involved.

I was raped in foster care because my foster mom refused to acknowledge the actions of her husband. She ignored everything because she was more concerned about getting her money than what happened to me. I hated her, and my mother more, for sitting by and letting this happen. People owe it to their families to speak up when they see such behavior from a relative. They need to help the child or children involved.

Some Misconceptions

Many people believe that abuse and neglect only happens in poor families or those of single moms. While it may be less apparent in more affluent neighborhoods, abuse and neglect exists across socio-economic lines. Abusive parents, even those with drug or alcohol problems, are found in all sorts of neighborhoods.

There is also the tendency to think that if someone was abused when they were young, then it's only natural that they will take it out on their children. This is certainly a misconception. I'm living testimony to that. Many people recognize how bad it was when they were young and want to do better, such as Annette in her story about her sister Nicole. Like me, she recognized how important it was to give a child a better life.

For those parents who are abusive, having been abused or neglected as a child does not give them a free pass to be abusive or neglectful to their children. "Hey, this is how my mother or father treated me." Although widely used, this is not an acceptable excuse. - **Deadbeat Moms Who Owe Money,** Yes, this is where we started, way back in Chapter 1. You need to track them down and get the police on the case. Many attorneys and courts say they are making a more concerted effort to go after women with the same intensity that they go after the men. Many men raising children alone and seeing no support from deadbeat moms don't believe them.

One of the problems seems to be the double standard where a man cannot be unemployed if he owes child support, while a woman can be unemployed. Men have written about the situation whereby they lose their job and are hauled off to jail for not paying child support.

"Well how am I supposed to look for another job and pay child support if you throw me in jail?" asked one exasperated father who had every intention of paying but no longer had any income.

Other fathers complain that they are busting their butts trying to hold down a job, support their kids and be there for them while the moms contribute nothing because they aren't working at the moment.

"You don't see them being thrown in jail for not having a job and not paying child support," says an angry dad.

One visitor to my website wrote me a note about her fiancé who has custody of his two teenage boys and is owed $35,000 in child support. She also comments that the woman (the deadbeat mom of the two boys) "Has not been made to get a job, serve jail time, or even been brought to court by Child Support Enforcement." Clearly there are still deadbeat moms who know how to beat the system.

Legislators need to hear from you if you believe that a mom should be held accountable for child expenses. The more people who write letters, gather signatures, send petitions to legislators and speak up to those who have the power in the courts, the more likely it is this double standard can be changed. As I mentioned earlier in the book, as women we are fighting for equal pay for the same jobs that men hold, and we certainly deserve it. However, the other side of equality means equal responsibility for child support. This battle needs more attention in the media and more support by the court system.

If you know of a deadbeat mom situation, please feel free to contact the website at www.deadbeatmomstories.com.

Giving Praise

I would like to give a shout out to all the parents, grandparents and stepparents that are looking out for, and protecting, the children. I know that it's not an easy task but they need you all. There will be plenty of sacrifices and plenty of hard times, but in the end they will thank you for everything you have done for them.

I know it's not fair for one parent to be left taking care of all the responsibilities of the child while the other parent has left the family and acts as if they do not have any children. However, we have to try hard to find forgiveness in our hearts for them. Otherwise the anger and frustration we feel towards them will always be hanging over our heads.

Moms are wonderful parents but dads are great parents too, if you find that times are a bit stressful for you and the father wants to take care of your children in his home let him until you can get yourself together. Parents should be able to work out visitation and financial support on their own. But if both parents fall short of money then both of you should show that child/children some much more love, remember love can never be replaced by money.

If there is anyone who would like to post a "thumbs up" to a single parent, to grandparents or to someone else who is taking care of someone else's child, or children, please go to my website (www.deadbeatmomstories. com) and let them know that they are doing a great job.

I want to thank you all for reading the book and if you know of a child that's being abused, call one of the numbers in the Appendix or the local police department.

Appendix

Childhelp® is a national organization that provides crisis assistance and other counseling and referral services. The Childhelp National Child Abuse Hotline is staffed 24 hours a day, 7 days a week, with professional crisis counselors who have access to a database of 55,000 emergency, social service, and support resources. All calls are anonymous. Contact them at 1-800-4-A-CHILD (1.800-422-4453).

These are some national websites and phone numbers you should know about. They provide data about child abuse and neglect studies as well as access to information that can benefit families.

National Child Welfare Websites:
Child Trends - childtrends.org - Includes Research, data and analysis from studies on children at all stages of development.

Child Welfare Information Gateway - childwelfare.gov - Information and resources to help protect children and strengthen families

Child Welfare League of America - cwla.org / Call: 202-688-4200 - Major coalition of hundreds of private and public agencies serving vulnerable children and families

Fostering Court Improvement: fosteringcourtimprovement.org / Call: 773-848-6880 - Organization committed to providing every state in the nation a platform of shared data from which the Dependency Court and the Child Welfare Agency can manage systems expressly designed to improve outcomes for children and families.

FRIENDS – friendsnrc.org - Family Resource Information, Education and Network Development Services serves as a resource to those programs and to the rest of the Child Abuse Prevention community.

The Judges' Page of National CASA: .casaforchildren.org/site - Online newsletter published by the National CASA Association and the National Council of Juvenile and Family Court Judges

National CASA Association – casaforchildren.org – Call 800-628-3233

- The National CASA Association is a network of 946 programs that are recruiting, training and supporting volunteers to represent the best interests of abused and neglected children in the courtroom and in other settings

National Child Traumatic Stress Network - nctsnet.org – They provide tools and materials to help child welfare administrators, caseworkers, and frontline staff understand and respond to the needs of traumatized children National Council of Juvenile & Family Court Judges - ncjfcj.org – Network of judges formed 75 years ago to improve the effectiveness of the nation's juvenile courts. They sought to address the following issues including child abuse and neglect, adoption and foster care, juvenile justice, family violence, victims of juvenile offenders, etc.

Prevent Child Abuse America - preventchildabuse.org - National organization working to prevent child abuse and neglect

Visiting a state's child abuse website will also help you learn about mandatory child abuse reporting laws that you may be subject to.

Also remember that if you think that a child is in immediate danger from child abuse or neglect then you should call 911.

Anyone can report suspected child abuse or neglect. Reporting abuse or neglect can protect a child and get help for a family—it may even save a child's life. In some States, any person who suspects child abuse or neglect is required to report.

If you suspect a child is being abused or neglected, or if you are a child who is being maltreated, contact your local child protective services office or law enforcement agency so professionals can assess the situation. Many States have a toll-free number to call to report suspected child abuse or neglect.

The state listing below is provided by Child Welfare Information Gateway.

Alabama
Local (toll): (334) 242-1310
(800-422-4453)
http://dhr.alabama.gov/services/Child_Protective_Services/Abuse_Neglect_ Reporting.aspx

Alaska
Toll-Free: (800) 478-4444
www.hss.state.ak.us/ocs/default.htm

Arizona
Toll-Free: (888) SOS-CHILD (888-767-2445)
www.azdes.gov/dcyf/cps/reporting.asp

Arkansas
Toll-Free: (800) 482-5964
http://www.arkansas.gov/reportARchildabuse/

California
Toll Free: (800-543-7993)
www.dss.cahwnet.gov/cdssweb/PG20.htm

Colorado

Local(toll):(303)412-5212
www.colorado.gov/cs/Satellite/CDHS-ChildYouthFam/CBON/1251590165629

Connecticut

Toll-Free: (800) 842-2288

www.state.ct.us/dcf/HOTLINE.htm

Delaware

Toll-Free: (800) 842-2288

http://kids.delaware.gov/services/crisis.shtml

District of Columbia

Local (toll): (202) 671-SAFE (202-671-7233)

http://cfsa.dc.gov/DC/CFSA/Support+the+Safety+Net/Report+Child+Abuse+and+Neglect

Florida

Toll-Free: (800) 96-ABUSE (800-962-2873)

www.dcf.state.fl.us/abuse/

Georgia

Toll-Free: (800) 422-4453

Hawaii
Local(toll):(808)933-0331
www.hawaii.gov/dhs/protection/social_services/child_welfare/

Idaho
TDD: (208) 332-7205
Toll-Free: (800) 926-2588

Illinois
Toll-Free: (800) 252-2873
Local (toll): (312) 814-6800

Indiana
Toll-Free: (800) 800-5556
www.in.gov/dcs/protection/dfcchi.html

Iowa
Toll-Free: (800) 362-2178

Kansas
Toll-Free: (800) 766-3777
www.srskansas.org/services/child_protective_services.htm

Kentucky
Toll-Free: (877) 597-2331
http://chfs.ky.gov/dcbs/dpp/childsafety.htm

Louisiana
Toll-Free: (855) 452-5437
http://dss.louisiana.gov/index.cfm?md=pagebuilder&tmp=home&pid=109

Maine
TTY: (800) 963-9490
Toll-Free: (800) 452-1999
www.maine.gov/dhhs/ocfs/hotlines.htm

Maryland
Toll-Free: (800) 422-4453
www.dhr.state.md.us/blog/?page_id=3973

Massachusetts
Toll-Free: (800) 792-5200
www.mass.gov/eohhs/consumer/family-services/child-abuse-neglect/

Michigan
Toll-Free: (855) 444-3911
Fax: (616) 977-1154
(616) 977-1158
www.michigan.gov/dhs/0,1607,7-124-5452_7119---,00.html

Minnesota
Toll-Free (800) 422-4453)

Mississippi
Toll-Free: (800) 222-8000
Local(toll):(601)359-4991
www.mdhs.state.ms.us/fcs_prot.html

Missouri
Toll-Free: (800) 392-3738
www.dss.mo.gov/cd/rptcan.htm

Montana
Toll-Free: (866) 820-5437
www.dphhs.mt.gov/cfsd/index.shtml

Nebraska
Toll-Free: (800) 252-4202
http://www.hhs.state.ne.us/cha/chaindex.htm

Nevada
Toll-Free: (800) 992-5757
http://dcfs.state.nv.us/DCFS_ReportSuspectedChildAbuse.htm

New Hampshire
Toll-Free: (800) 894-5533
Local(toll):(603)271-6556
www.dhhs.state.nh.us/dcyf/cps/contact.htm

New Jersey
Toll-Free: (877) 652-2873
TDD: (800) 835-5510
TTY: (800) 835-5510
www.nj.gov/dcf/reporting/how/index.html

New Mexico
Toll-Free: (855) 333-7233
www.cyfd.org/content/reporting-abuse-or-neglect

New York
Toll-Free: (800) 342-3720
TDD: (800) 369-2437
Local(toll):(518)474-8740 www.ocfs.state.ny.us/main/cps/

North Carolina
Toll-Free: (800) 422-4453
http://www.dhhs.state.nc.us/dss/cps/index.htm

North Dakota
Toll-Free (800) 245-3736
www.nd.gov/dhs/services/childfamily/cps/#reporting

Ohio
Toll-Free (800) 686-1556
http://jfs.ohio.gov/county/cntydir.stm

Oklahoma
Toll-Free: (800) 522-3511
www.okdhs.org/programsandservices/cps/default.htm

Oregon
Toll-Free: (800) 646-5430
www.oregon.gov/DHS/children/abuse/cps/report.shtml

Pennsylvania
Toll-Free: (800) 932-0313
TDD: (866) 872-1677

Puerto Rico
Toll-Free: (800) 981-8333
Local (toll): (787) 749-1333

Rhode Island
Toll-Free: (800) RI-CHILD (800-742-4453)
www.dcyf.ri.gov/child_welfare/index.php

South Carolina
Local(toll):(803)898-7601
http://dss.sc.gov/content/customers/protection/cps/index.aspx

South Dakota
Toll-Free: (800) 227-3020
http://dss.sd.gov/cps/protective/reporting.asp

Tennessee
Toll-Free: (877) 237-0004
https://reportabuse.state.tn.us/

Texas
Department of Family and Protective Services Toll-Free: (800) 252-5400
www.dfps.state.tx.us/Contact_Us/report_abuse.asp
Spanish: www.dfps.state.tx.us/Espanol/default.asp

Utah
Toll-Free: (855) 323-3237
www.hsdcfs.utah.gov

Vermont
(800)649-5285
www.dcf.state.vt.us/fsd/reporting_child_abuse

Virginia
Toll-Free: (800) 552-7096
Local(toll):(804)786-8536
www.dss.virginia.gov/family/cps/index.html

Washington
(866) END-HARM (866-363-4276)
TTY: (800) 624-6186
Toll-Free: (800) 562-5624
www1.dshs.wa.gov/ca/safety/abuseReport.asp?2

West Virginia
Toll-Free: (800) 352-6513
www.wvdhhr.org/bcf/children_adult/cps/report.asp

Wisconsin
Toll-Free (608) 267-3905
http://dcf.wisconsin.gov/children/CPS/cpswimap.HTM

Wyoming
Toll-Free (307) 777-7561
http://dfsweb.state.wy.us/protective-services/cps/index.html

INDEX

Books on Collecting Child Support

How to Collect Child Support, 3rd Edition
By Geraldine Jensen, a leading child advocate, former welfare mom and founder of the Association for Children for Enforcement of Support Smarter Changes, 2006

Rightfully Yours: Past-due child support, alimony, & securing your share of your ex's pension.

By Gary Shulman, attorney who specializes in domestic relations issues Self-Counsel Press, Inc.; 1 edition, 2003
Additional Notes:
Families more likely to have child abuse and/or neglect include:

- Families in which there is domestic violence among adults
- Families in which there is alcohol and/or drug abuse.
- Parents or adults in the home with untreated mental illness
- One-parent families in which the parent is both working and raising children, creating a high level of stress.
- Parents who lack the necessary parenting skills, which may include teens or parents from abusive or neglectful home.

In all of the above cases, therapy, groups or rehab programs dealing with the problem, social workers, classes or any other type of professional outside help can be beneficial.

Emotional Abuse

Not as obvious as physical abuse or neglect, emotional abuse can be very damaging to a child. See if someone you know exhibits the following behaviors toward their child, especially on an ongoing basis.

- Humiliating him/her in front of others
- Harassing
- Bullying
- Name calling or belittling.
- Threatening violence
- Indifference or ignoring
- Placing him/her in potentially dangerous situations Five

Questions to Ask about Yourself or Someone Else

1. Do you/they feel disconnected from your/their child?
2. Do you/they sometimes lose control and cannot stop hitting or yelling or both?
3. Do you/they feel that a child is interfering in your/their life?
4. Do other people comment to you/them about parenting skills?
5. Do you/they wish you/they did not have children?

If you answered yes to most or all of these questions, you or the person you are thinking or, may be a deadbeat mom. Seek out someone you know and trust, such as a close friend or family member, pastor or social worker to talk to.

It Takes a Village to Raise a Child

Taking care of children is almost impossible alone. If you are married, or in a serious relationship you should share some of the responsibilities. But, since many of us go it alone, it's important to make a list of people who can be your village. If you know someone whom you believe is overwhelmed and needs support, besides offering some yourself, you might help them make a list of a few people whom they could call for help. This can include a local babysitter, perhaps someone who could run errands for them or even any local programs that can watch a child after school or provide any helpful services.

Use the lines below to list some people and/or places that may be able to help you or someone else build your village. Remember, parents need support!

____

____

____

____

____

____

Suggestions for Talking with an Abused Child

It's not up to you to start talking to a child about abuse unless it is a child you already know, such as a family member. And even then, approach cautiously with a general conversation. For example, if you think the child is being neglected, you can tell them what you had for lunch or breakfast and ask what they had to eat. Often, your best opportunity to talk is when the child is engaged in a familiar activity like drawing for example.

If a child starts telling you about a family members or someone who has been abusive to them, your best reaction is to listen and let them tell you their story. If you act shocked, or get angry the child may think that he or she is doing something wrong and may get frightened.

It is hard for children to talk about such behavior, so if they do confide in you, be supportive and let them know it's okay to talk to you If you ask questions make them short simple questions and do not start an interrogation.

If you feel that the children may be putting themselves in danger by talking to you then do not continue the conversation, switch the subject.

If you are alarmed by what a child is telling you, do not react with the child present. If you feel that you should call protective services, do so away from the child or other family members.

About the Author

Naomi Brunner is a graduate of Monroe College in New York City. She spent four years at the Administration for Children's Services as a program coordinator. While at the ACS, she gained insight into the overload of cases backing up the system and why it takes so long for ACS to respond to families in need.

In recent years, while receiving her B.A. in Computer Information Systems, Naomi has worked for the Catholic Charities of Archdiocese, New York.

There she spent nearly six months as a Hurricane Katrina Operator, collecting client information needs and making referrals to specific social service agencies for case management and for posting with the agency

C.A.N. Along with fielding thousands of calls from people after the tragedy, she also maintained ongoing information and resource files and underwent training on specifics to Katrina case coordination. As a result of her efforts she received the NYC Direct Customer Service Award in 2006 from the New York Federal Executive Board of the Katrina Evacuee Inter- Agency Team.

Over the past twenty years, Naomi has also worked as a volunteer with agencies such as: Goldwater Memorial Hospital, Bronx Lebanon Hospital, Coler Memorial

Hospital, Family Dynamics Children's Center, the City Volunteer Corp., the Bernard Fineson Mental Health Center, and the Red Cross Emergency Center, to name a few.

"At times I used to wish I had a place for many children to stay when they were being abused. I helped the few that I could and I prayed for all of the other abused children in the world. Yet, I always felt like that wasn't enough. The more I watched the news, the more I began to hear about such stories, the more I wanted to find another way of getting the message across about deadbeat mothers. So, that is why I decided to write this book." Naomi Brunner

Contributor:

Dr. Simon Casey

Simon Casey Ph.D., (CADACII, CEDS) has over 20 years of experience as a therapist, consultant, speaker, author, and relationship expert. Casey
graduated from Waltham College in London with an emphasis on pre-med. He concluded alcoholism certification at the University of Irvine and later graduated from California Coast University with his Doctor of Psychology degree. In addition, he is a Board Certified Alcohol and Drug Abuse Counselor and Board Certified Eating Disorders Specialist.

Dr. Casey is quite familiar with deadbeat moms and the repercussions of their behavior on their children. Currently, Dr. Casey is the Executive Director of Med link Treatment Center in San Clemente California. The center specializes in addiction, medical detoxification, eating disorders and dual diagnosis, which refer to the presence of both mental health disorders and chemical dependency. Disorders such as depression, anxiety and bipolar combined with alcoholism and drug addiction create this dilemma. Deadbeat moms very often exemplify these.

He also teaches the Power of Emotions to groups and organizations as well as executives who want personal success, balance and an ethical work environment. His book, Secrets to Emotional Wealth: Follow your Yellow Brick Road, focuses on achieving success at a personal level.

Rich Mintzer: Also involved with this project is Rich Mintzer, an author and editor of numerous non-fiction books whom I met a couple of years ago. Rich helped me put this book together.

Ishan Ausmore: Book Model Photographed by Jackay.

Laura Tower: My Deadbeat Moms Website Designer

Samuel M: My Inspiration.

ʃ

This book is dedicated to my Grandmother Ann, may you rest in peace

ʃ

www.ingramcontent.com/pod-product-compliance
Lightning Source LLC
La Vergne TN
LVHW020057090426
835510LV00040B/2142

* 9 7 8 0 6 1 5 9 4 6 1 4 6 *